At Issue

Should Juveniles Be Given Life Without Parole?

Other Books in the At Issue Series:

At Issue

Should Juveniles Be Given Life Without Parole?

Olivia Ferguson, Book Editor

GREENHAVEN PRESS
A part of Gale, Cengage Learning

GALE
CENGAGE Learning

Detroit • New York • San Francisco • New Haven, Conn • Waterville, Maine • London

Christine Nasso, *Publisher*
Elizabeth Des Chenes, *Managing Editor*

© 2011 Greenhaven Press, a part of Gale, Cengage Learning.

Gale and Greenhaven Press are registered trademarks used herein under license.

For more information, contact:
Greenhaven Press
27500 Drake Rd.
Farmington Hills, MI 48331-3535
Or you can visit our Internet site at gale.cengage.com

For product information and technology assistance, contact us at

Gale Customer Support, 1-800-877-4253
For permission to use material from this text or product, submit all requests online at www.cengage.com/permissions.

Further permissions questions can be e-mailed to permissionrequest@cengage.com.

Articles in Greenhaven Press anthologies are often edited for length to meet page requirements. In addition, original titles of these works are changed to clearly present the main thesis and to explicitly indicate the author's opinion. Every effort is made to ensure that Greenhaven Press accurately reflects the original intent of the authors. Every effort has been made to trace the owners of copyrighted material.

Cover image copyright © Illustration Works.

LIBRARY OF CONGRESS CATALOGING-IN-PUBLICATION DATA

Should juveniles be given life without parole? / Olivia Ferguson, book editor.
      p. cm. -- (At issue)
   Includes bibliographical references and index.
   ISBN 978-0-7377-5165-9 (hardcover) -- ISBN 978-0-7377-5166-6 (pbk.)
   1. Juvenile corrections--United States. 2. Life imprisonment--United States.
I. Ferguson, Olivia.
   KF9820.S54 2011
   365'.608350973--dc22
                                                                   2011000874

Printed in the United States of America
1 2 3 4 5 6 7 15 14 13 12 11

Contents

Introduction

The Supreme Court's treatment of juveniles has evolved over time to reflect advances in understanding the unique characteristics of juvenile crimes and to ensure fair and equitable treatment under the law. Studies in child psychology have proven that children's minds are not as developed as adults'; therefore juveniles do not have the same decision-making capabilities as adults do and are more likely to succumb to their impulses. These studies have led to debate among lawmakers and the public about how children are handled in the courts and whether or not they should be held to a different standard than their adult counterparts.

The Supreme Court first reexamined juvenile law and the death penalty in *Thompson v. Oklahoma* in 1988. When he was fifteen, William Thompson murdered his brother-in-law. Although Oklahoma law dictated that Thompson should be tried in a juvenile court, the prosecution fought and won to try him as an adult. Thompson was convicted of first-degree murder and sentenced to death. The case was appealed to the Supreme Court, and the Court overturned the death sentence, which the majority found to be "cruel and unusual punishment" for juveniles under the age of sixteen, citing the Eighth and Fourteenth Amendments of the US Constitution. Instead of the death sentence, Thompson was sentenced to life without parole (LWOP).

The Court went a step further in 2005 when it banned the death penalty for juveniles altogether in *Roper v. Simmons*. When Christopher Simmons was seventeen, he and two younger friends planned and carried out the murder of Shirley Crook. They broke into her home, bound her hands and took her to a nearby park where they threw her from a train trestle into the river below. After his confession to the police, Simmons was sentenced to death. The case was appealed to the Supreme Court, and like *Thompson v. Oklahoma* the Court cited the Eighth and Fourteenth Amendments in its ruling that capital punishment for anyone under the age of eighteen amounted to cruel and unusual punishment and was therefore unconstitutional. Like Thompson, Simmons was sentenced to life without parole.

With the death penalty excluded from juvenile criminals, life without parole has become the strictest form of punishment for juveniles, and the constitutionality of that sentence has come under debate. Many opponents of life without parole claim that it also falls under the Eighth Amendment clause of cruel and unusual punishment. James Ridgeway and Jean Casella, in their 2010 *Mother Jones* article "When Punishing Teens Is Cruel and Unusual," liken life without parole for juveniles to solitary confinement because "a large number of young offenders end up in long-term isolation in adult prisons, either because they are considered disciplinary problems, because they feel compelled to join prison gangs, or because they have to be isolated from adult offenders 'for their own protection.'"

Proponents of life without parole often contend that it is wrong to cause victims and their families the trauma of parole hearings. In the article "House Committee Debates Eliminating Life Without Parole Sentences for Youth," Michael Novinson quotes Jennifer Bishop-Jenkins, a victim and opponent of the elimination of life without parole sentences for juveniles, who believes that attending parole hearings and reopening "this pain every three years, for the rest of our lives, and perhaps those of our children, is quite literally torture."

There are many factors to consider when debating the issue of life without parole. The following viewpoints include arguments from the proponents as well as the opponents in an attempt to provide a wide range of views on the topic. Also included is a list of other articles and books for further reading, as well as a list of organizations that can be contacted for more information.

1

The Supreme Court Ruling on Juvenile LWOP Rebalances the Justice System

Andrew Cohen

Andrew Cohen is the legal affairs columnist for Politics Daily *as well as the chief legal analyst and legal editor for CBS News Ra-*

*lly made the decision to stop the
ole (LWOP) for juveniles who are
es. This decision is restoring some
at had taken its power too far and
at many have argued are a direct
nusual punishment" clause of the
e Court justice Anthony Kennedy
ugh-on-crime movement had gone
percentage of districts actually im-
ent juvenile offenders. Many oppo-
e fight to have the decision over-
e the ones who, through advocating
ision in the first place.*

urt declared Monday [May 17,
ffenders could no longer be sen-
thout parole [LWOP] for crimes
closed a legal loop that had been
40 years in the making. It is the typical American story of

Andrew Cohen, "Juvenile Justice: Anthony Kennedy, Supreme Court Right an Old Wrong," *Politics Daily*, May 19, 2010. Reproduced by permission.

power, overreaching and short-sightedness—but also a wonderful example of how well our legal system was built for balance, like a pendulum that never goes too far in any one direction.

Extremist Lawmakers Must Be Reined In

The ruling reminds us that even the most concentrated and relentless political forces of the past generation—what you might call the "law and order" lobby—ultimately must abate at the walls of the Constitution. It is a reaction, a correction, from the highest level of lawgiver to check just one of the unlawful and unbecoming imbalances of power that have been building within the criminal justice system, decade after decade, layered up brick by brick by politicians, lawyers and lower court judges.

For years now, these keystones of the justice system have gotten comfortable (and, where applicable, re-elected) by tickling the "tough on crime" fancies of their constituents. It's been an easy movement to join, defend and legislate for. You argue for the prosecution of more crimes and for the tougher, longer sentences upon conviction. You argue for infrequent (or nonexistent) parole. You argue that kids who commit "adult" crimes ought to be treated like adults. And if anyone on the other side argues with you, you simply call them "soft" on crime, and thus a coward, and thus dangerous to have around the policy-making machine. These people put the emphasis on the "order" in "law and order."

The most recent iteration of this movement started with [President] Richard Nixon's angry and silent majority [those Nixon refferred to in a 1969 speech who, though a majority, do not openly express their opinions]. It was given a symbol in 1971 with [actor] Clint Eastwood's "Dirty Harry" [movies]. It was given legs through the rise of victims' rights groups all through the 1970s and 1980s. It benefited greatly from the end of the [chief justice Earl] Warren court [which expanded civil liberties and judicial power] and the rise of the [chief justice William] Rehnquist court [which favored states' rights]. It was carried along on the back of the [President Ronald] Reagan Revolution, past Willie Horton [a convicted felon who during a weekend furlough program committed robbery and rape], and into the O.J. Simpson [where Simpson was acquitted of murder] trial, where it was eventually rechanneled into the spirit and voice of [television host] Nancy Grace, the archangel of retribution. It is part posse, part practical, and evidently wholly American.

Justice Anthony Kennedy declared that the [tough-on-crime] movement had finally gone too far—that its overreaching had crossed the boundary into unconstitutional cruelty.

Lobbyists Have Disregarded Expert Opinion

Indeed, the primary legal issue presented by *Graham v. Florida*—does the Constitution permit these life sentences for juvenile offenders—was generated directly by the tough-on-crime movement's success in ensuring longer and longer sentences for younger and younger criminals. For decades now, the lobby and its tribunes have accomplished this harsh goal by foolishly forsaking juvenile justice systems. They have done it by shallowly mocking the bona fides of mental health experts and civil libertarians. They have done it to prevent crime, but in doing so with such zealotry have also filled to overflowing America's prisons, giving the nation the dubious distinction of being the "most incarcerated" one on Earth.

In his majority opinion Monday, Justice Anthony Kennedy declared that the movement had finally gone too far—that its overreaching had crossed the boundary into unconstitutional cruelty. He found in the record of the case (and convinced at least four of his colleagues to so find) that America is actually turning its back on its current juvenile sentencing policies. He won over the court with a brilliant twist. He simply changed the standard of measurement to be used in determining where the "national consensus" may be on the topic of juvenile sentencing and the Eighth Amendment. The new rule: It's not what you've got—it's how you use it.

Not All States Use Juvenile LWOP

As Justice Clarence Thomas would point out in dissent, no fewer than 37 states, Congress and the District of Columbia all *permit* life sentences without parole for juveniles who have not been convicted of murder. That didn't matter, Justice Kennedy argued. What matters is what those jurisdictions were *doing* with the power to render those longer sentences for juveniles. And what he found was that only "12 jurisdictions nationwide in fact impose life without parole sentences on juvenile non-homicide offenders—and most of those impose the sentence quite rarely—while 26 states as well as the District of Columbia do not impose them despite apparent statutory authorization."

The mere presence of long-sentence statutes on the books, Kennedy wrote, wasn't dispositive. "Many states have chosen to move away from juvenile court systems and to allow juveniles to be transferred to, or charged directly in, adult court," he wrote. ". . . Once [there] a juvenile offender may receive the same sentence as would be given to an adult offender, including a life without parole sentence. But the fact that transfer and direct charging laws make life without parole possible for some juvenile non-homicide offenders does not justify a judgment that many states intended to subject such offenders to life without parole sentences."

Convicted Juveniles Finally Have Hope

Thus does the pendulum swing back. "Hopeless" sentences for juveniles not convicted of murder will go the way of the death penalty for juvenile murders. *Both* types of sentences, Justice Kennedy wrote, violate the "cruel and unusual" punishment clause of the Eighth Amendment. The "law and order" types already are angry and lobbing the old soft-on-crime charges. But this time they have no one to blame but themselves. They went too far and, on Monday, they were reined in by a Supreme Court justice, a Reagan appointee, who is relentlessly building his own legal legacy as an unlikely defender of a still-recognizable strain of genuine juvenile justice.

2

The Supreme Court Ruling Raises Concern for the Future of Juvenile LWOP

John Richards

John Richards is a writer for LegalMatch.com.

Over time the US Supreme Court has placed limits on the use of the death penalty. The Court has now considered whether or not juveniles should be sentenced to life without parole (LWOP). They have ruled that life without parole may not be given to a juvenile unless their crime involves murder. With restrictions already placed on the death sentence, retaining the possibility of life without parole is important. Society needs an "ultimate punishment" for those who commit heinous crimes and also as a deterrent. The Court's decision should encourage those who run prisons to focus on rehabilitation, as more people will eventually be up for parole.

Since the death penalty was reinstated by the Supreme Court in 1976, after a brief moratorium that began in 1972, that same court has significantly limited situations in which it can be used.

In 1977, the Supreme Court held that it was unconstitutional for the death penalty to be used in the case involving the rape of an adult, where the victim did not die, leaving open the question of whether or not the rape of a child is still eligible for the death penalty.

John Richards, "After Limits on Death Penalty, Is Life Without Parole Next?" Legal Match.com, June 2, 2010. Reproduced by permission.

In 2008, the Supreme Court ruled on that question, holding that the rape of a child is not a crime eligible for the death penalty, where the victim did not die. This effectively means that, as of 2008, murder is the only crime eligible for the death penalty, with the possible exception of treason, and some crimes within the military justice system (mutiny, desertion in time of war, etc.), which is completely separate from the civilian criminal justice system.

Only mentally competent adults who committed murder ... can be constitutionally put to death.

In addition to limiting the crimes eligible for the death penalty to an extremely narrow category, the U.S. Supreme Court has also limited who the death penalty can be used against, irrespective of the crimes they committed. In 2002, the Supreme Court held that it was unconstitutional to execute people who are mentally retarded (generally defined as having an IQ below 70). In 2005, the same court held that states cannot execute anyone who was under the age of 18 at the time the crime was committed.

This leaves us with a good idea of where the death penalty in the U.S. currently stands: only mentally competent adults who committed murder (almost always with some aggravating factor) can be constitutionally put to death.

The Supreme Court Limits Juvenile LWOP

It looks like the Supreme Court is now ready to consider limits on another controversial "ultimate punishment"—life imprisonment without the possibility of parole [LWOP]. The Supreme Court handed down a decision in the case of *Graham v. Florida*, holding that individuals who are under 18 (at the time the crime was committed) cannot be sentenced to life without the possibility of parole in crimes where the victim did not die.

It's important to note that this decision does not mandate the eventual release of a minor who is sentenced to life in prison; it simply says that they must eventually be eligible for parole. If the state parole board finds that this person remains a threat to society, he or she can be imprisoned indefinitely. The court wasn't clear on the constitutionality of sentences that amount to life without parole, but go by another name, such as a 200-year prison sentence with parole possible after 150 years, or something similar.

This decision does not mandate the eventual release of a minor who is sentenced to life in prison.

Now, this is an extremely narrow ruling. It only applies to minors when they commit crimes other than homicide. So, adults who commit serious non-homicide crimes can still get life without parole, as can minors who commit homicide.

The Court cited some pretty good reasons for its decision—the brains of adolescents are not fully developed, and there is no way to determine with complete accuracy whether or not they can eventually be rehabilitated. Furthermore, the decision leaves open the option to keep someone locked up for life if they do, in fact, prove to be irredeemably depraved, even if they were a minor when they committed the crime. All that this ruling says is that a minor who commits a non-homicide crime must eventually be given some opportunity to prove that they have been rehabilitated. If they fail to prove that, then they can stay in jail for life.

This rule, if the restrictions stop here, seems personally reasonable. I hope however, that life in prison without parole remains available for the most heinous of crimes. While not quite as final and irrevocable as the death penalty, life without parole is a very, very severe punishment, and should not be imposed lightly. If the U.S. eventually abolishes the death penalty, there will need to be some "ultimate punishment."

Society Needs the LWOP Sentence

Life without the possibility of parole is, for the most part, an ultimate punishment. Modern high-security prisons make escape exceedingly difficult and rare, meaning that a sentence of life without parole has largely the same effect (in terms of removing a dangerous criminal from society) as the death penalty. Life without parole has further advantages over the death penalty—a person serving that sentence can be released if they're eventually exonerated. Of course, this can't undo the time that a wrongfully convicted person spent in prison, but considering that we can't bring people back from the dead, it's much better than post-hoc exoneration of a person who's been executed.

However, I don't believe that complete abolition of the sentence of life without parole (for any class of people) is the way to go, either. Like any severe punishment, it needs to be applied judiciously, and reserved for the most severe crimes, but I believe that it is in some cases necessary.

While no punishment, including the death penalty, will deter all crime, there's no doubt that it deters *some* would-be criminals. And it's indisputable that these punishments deter the individuals they're used on, simply by making it impossible to repeat them.

Focus on Rehabilitating Juveniles

Finally, while sentencing with an eye toward retribution may be satisfying on some base emotional level, it is probably not the best policy on which to base a justice system. The focus, especially with juvenile offenders, should be rehabilitation. If most juvenile convicts must now be made eligible for parole eventually, perhaps those who run prisons will begin to think more about what types of people they want to release. Do we want to release hardened criminals who have lost decades of their life, and probably have nothing to lose? Or do we want to release people who, while incarcerated, have acquired new and useful skills, learned to read, or otherwise bettered themselves?

While some people are beyond rehabilitation, a fact which this decision acknowledges and accommodates, I believe that a significant percentage can be rehabilitated.

Perhaps this decision will force authorities to think about that possibility.

3

Cases Must Be Considered Individually When Sentencing Juveniles

Michael Kirkland

Michael Kirkland is a journalist for UPI.com, a part of United Press International.

Many questions arise regarding the debate over juvenile life without parole; among them is whether each case should be considered individually, according to the severity of the crime and the age of the juvenile when he commits it. Two such cases under deliberation are those of Terrence Graham and Joe Harris Sullivan, both with very different circumstances to consider. The main issue with these cases is that one juvenile was only thirteen at the time he committed his crime and the other was seventeen, which raises the debate of the culpability between the two. While the fight against sentencing to death those juveniles who committed murder has been won, many still feel that life without parole sentences for these young people are just as bad.

Every once in a while society pauses to take stock, usually through the courts, to see if its actions measure up to "evolving standards of decency."

The U.S. Supreme Court takes up the gauntlet Monday [November 9, 2009,] when it hears two Florida cases involving penalties handed out to juveniles. At issue: Is it constitutional to sentence someone to life in prison for a non-homicide committed when the defendant was a juvenile?

Michael Kirkland, "US Supreme Court: Life Without Parole for a 13-year-old," UPI.com, November 8, 2009. Reproduced by permission.

Lawyers commenting on the cases refer to the punishment as "LWOP"—not a slur on our Italian-American heritage but an acronym for "life without parole."

Is LWOP appropriate for a repeatedly violent 17-year-old? If appropriate for a 17-year-old, is it appropriate for a 13-year-old, like the violator in one of the Florida cases?

Many conservatives argue it is up to the states and their lawmakers—not the courts—to decide the "evolving standards of decency."

If the thought of LWOP for children offends you—is there really a difference between execution and sentencing someone to die behind bars 60 or 70 years after a conviction—should the brutality of a juvenile's crimes influence the severity of his or her penalty? What if a judge believes a juvenile is irredeemable and on a path that sooner or later will lead to murder?

And what about the wishes of the public? Many conservatives argue it is up to the states and their lawmakers—not the courts—to decide the "evolving standards of decency." Legislatures across the country have been constructing harsh penalties to combat the emergence of juvenile "super predators," the *ABA Journal* reports.

The two cases before the high court present strikingly different facts.

Considering Each Case Individually

Joe Harris Sullivan was 13 in 1989 when he and several older juveniles burglarized an elderly woman's house in Pensacola. Prosecutors say he went back after the burglary and sexually attacked her so savagely, he severely injured her.

Prisoner advocates such as the Equal Justice Initiative say Sullivan is one of only two 13-year-olds in the United States sentenced to life without parole for an offense that did not involve a homicide, he was "fingered" by the older defendants (who served brief sentences), identified by the victim only by voice and the DNA evidence from his rape charge was destroyed by officials before it could be used as evidence. The group says Sullivan is mentally retarded and now in a wheelchair.

Sullivan is black and his victim was white.

Terrance Graham was 16 when he pleaded guilty to armed robbery with assault or battery (an offense that could carry a life sentence) and robbery of a restaurant in which a fellow defendant hit the manager over the head with a steel pipe. The plea was conditional on Graham spending a year in detention and three years on probation.

He was released in June 2004. By the following December Graham at 17 was conducting a home invasion in which he and two others forced a man to the floor and Graham held a pistol to the man's head, demanding money.

After his arrest, Graham admitted committing several other robberies in the same neighborhood. On conviction, he was sentenced to life without parole for violating his parole.

Like Sullivan, Graham is black. His victims were white and Hispanic.

Now, unless the Supreme Court steps in, Sullivan and Graham are likely to die in prison.

Luckily for them, the high court has been moving steadily toward jurisprudence that takes into account the relationship between a criminal's ability to be responsible for a crime and the severity of a sentence.

Other Similar Cases Used in the Defense

In 2002's *Atkins vs. Virginia*, the Supreme Court ruled 6-3 the Eighth Amendment's ban on cruel and unusual punishment should be seen in terms of the "evolving standards of decency that mark the progress of a maturing society," and that the execution of mentally retarded inmates was unconstitutional.

In contrast, the high court had to make its way gradually toward banning executions for those who had committed homicides when they were minors.

After a plurality of justices decided in 1988's *Thompson vs. Oklahoma* that those who committed murder before the age of 16 could not be executed, a narrow majority decided the next year a defendant who killed when 15 or 16 could be executed.

Then came 2005's *Roper vs. Simmons*. In that case, a 5-4 majority concluded the Eighth Amendment, applied to the states by the use of the 14th Amendment, banned the execution of all those who committed murder before the age of 18.

Ashley Nellis, research analyst for the Sentencing Project in Washington, [D.C.,] told the *ABA Journal*: "Striking down juvenile LWOP sentences is a natural evolution from the *Roper* decision. It hopefully would reverse some of the policies over the last few decades that were overly punitive with respect to juvenile defendants."

Lyle Denniston, dean emeritus of the Supreme Court press corps, the only person to earn a plaque in the high court press room, has speculated the justices may take divergent paths in disposing of the cases.

The Equal Justice Initiative, in a friend-of-the-court brief in support of Sullivan, . . . says 13- and 14-year-olds as a class are much less mature than 17-year-olds.

Writing for Scotusblog.com, Denniston says "there is at least a chance that Sullivan might not be allowed to raise his constitutional argument, because it could be found to have come too late." Sullivan didn't raise his constitutional argument until 20 years after his conviction.

However, Sullivan's lawyers, he points out, aim their arguments specifically to those sentenced to life in prison without parole for a crime committed when a violator was 13—suggesting that a 13-year-old is far less responsible than a 17-year-old.

The Equal Justice Initiative, in a friend-of-the-court brief in support of Sullivan, says "nationwide . . . only 73 such sentences (for those under 14) have been imposed in a quarter of a million cases where they could have been," adding "13- and 14-year-olds as a class are much less mature than 17-year-olds," the *Journal* reported.

If Sullivan doesn't pan out, the justices could still make a constitutional finding in Graham.

Roper Ruling May Be Prophetic Here

Roper vs. Simmons, out of Missouri, offers a glimpse at how the court may rule in at least one of the Florida juvenile cases. Justice Anthony Kennedy, a key moderate swing vote who remains on the court, wrote the 5-4 majority opinion in *Roper*, concluding that the execution of those committing a murder before age 18 was unconstitutional.

The numbers bode well for Graham and Sullivan as well. Only retired Justice David Souter is missing from the four-member liberal bloc that joined Kennedy to form the narrow majority. His place has been taken by Justice Sonia Sotomayor, also likely to vote in concert with the liberals.

When a juvenile commits a heinous crime the state cannot extinguish his life and his potential to attain a mature understanding of his own humanity.

In the *Roper* minority, moderate conservative Justice Sandra Day O'Connor has been succeeded by conservative Justice Samuel Alito.

In other words, the 5-4 *Roper* court remains ideologically intact.

And Kennedy's words in writing the majority opinion in *Roper* seem prophetic as to how he might write in at least one of the Florida cases, whether the majority rules for or against the two men:

> "Although the (Supreme) Court cannot deny or overlook the brutal crimes too many juvenile offenders have committed, it disagrees with (Missouri's) contention that, given the court's own insistence on individualized consideration in capital sentencing, it is arbitrary and unnecessary to adopt a categorical rule barring imposition of the death penalty on an offender under 18," Kennedy wrote. "An unacceptable likelihood exists that the brutality or cold-blooded nature of any particular crime would overpower mitigating arguments based on youth as a matter of course, even where the juvenile offender's objective immaturity, vulnerability and lack of true depravity should require a sentence less severe than death. When a juvenile commits a heinous crime, the state can exact forfeiture of some of the most basic liberties, but the state cannot extinguish his life and his potential to attain a mature understanding of his own humanity."

Predictably, the Graham and Sullivan cases have evoked a large coterie of supporters, including religious organizations, celebrities and nuns.

4

LWOP for Juveniles
Is Morally Wrong

John Coleman

John Coleman is a contributor to America, *a Roman Catholic weekly magazine.*

The 1990s produced a rush of legislation to curb perceived crime, with lawmakers and politicians becoming tougher on crime to benefit their political agendas. States passed laws allowing juveniles to be tried as adults as well as habitual offender laws, allowing juveniles who repeatedly committed crimes to be given a sentence of life without parole (LWOP). The sentence is being tested before the Supreme Court. Those arguing against LWOP cite that giving a juvenile a life sentence with no chance of parole is cruel and unusual punishment, according to the Constitution. Juveniles are not as mentally capable as adults and are more likely to act on impulse and fall prey to peer pressure, which is why they should be treated differently than adults.

I was recently asked to write a "white paper" draft [a report addressing an issue and ideas for solving it] for the California Catholic Bishops for possible voting on the issue of life-sentence without parole for juveniles. The United States Supreme Court, currently, is adjudicating two petitions from incarcerated prisoners from the State of Florida who were sentenced to life-sentences without parole when they were, respectively, thirteen and sixteen years old. Neither was guilty of

John Coleman, "Life Without Parole for Juveniles: Morally Wrong," *America Magazine*, April 13, 2010. Reproduced by permission of America Press. For subscription information, visit www.americamagazine.org.

homicide or a felony-murder crime, although they had committed armed robbery or rape. The Court will be determining whether life-sentence for a juvenile who has not committed a homicide or a felony-murder crime constitutes a disproportionately cruel and unusual punishment—by reason of age—under the Eighth Amendment to the United States Constitution. In 2005, a narrowly divided Court ruled the death penalty for juveniles unconstitutional (*Roper versus Simmons*). In 2002, (*Atkins versus Virginia*), the Court also outlawed the death penalty for mentally disabled offenders.

Among the *amici* briefs [written by "friends" of the court who are not party to the case but have expert opinions to offer] in favor of the petitioners are supporting arguments against life-sentence without parole for juveniles from several Catholic organizations (The American Catholic Correctional Chaplains Association; the Archdiocese of Los Angeles—but, to my surprise, not from the U.S. Catholic Conference [of Bishops]). Currently, 109 prisoners in the United States are serving life-sentences without parole for non-homicide offenses, committed as juveniles; 77 of them are in Florida.

Many States Are Not Using This Sentence

A number of states (Texas, Colorado) have, legislatively, recently rescinded life-sentence without parole for juveniles, even in cases which involved homicide or felony murder charges. In these two states, however, there are provisions for life sentence for juveniles which only allow a possible parole after 40 years in prison. A bill proposing a similar outlawing of life-sentence without parole for juveniles is now pending before the California Assembly. California has 239 prisoners who were sentenced to life-sentences without parole as juveniles. Nationally the number runs to 1,755.

To some extent, the spike in life-sentences (for adults and juveniles) after the mid-1980's (there are 140,610 prisoners presently serving life-sentences—41,095 without possibility of parole, compared to only 34,000 in 1984), came from a perceived rise in crime in the early 1990's. States passed habitual offender laws (three or two strikes and you are out!), mandated mandatory minimum sentences which lessened judicial discretion in sentencing and put sentencing decisions more in the hands of legislators and prosecutors. States passed laws which facilitated the transfer of juvenile offenders to adult courts.

Political rhetoric of the 1990's, at times, referred to juvenile offenders as "super-predators" and mouthed slogans such as "adult crime, adult time." Every state permits life sentences for juveniles. Forty-five states allow life-sentences without parole for juveniles. In some cases of felony-murder, passive accomplices (e.g., "look-outs" in armed robberies) who had no idea a homicide was going to occur and did not directly wield any weapon have received life-sentences without parole.

Every other country has banned life-sentence without parole for juveniles. The argument against life-sentence without parole for juveniles parallels, closely, the argument of the majority in *Roper versus Simmons*. Conservative lawyers oppose extending *Roper versus Simmons* in a way which precludes life-sentence without parole for juveniles. They argue, "death" is different. But *Roper versus Simmons* also argued that children are different.

[Juveniles] are more given to impulsivity, recklessness and are more susceptible to peer pressure.

Juveniles Can Be Rehabilitated

Juveniles have not developed in the same way as adults. They are more given to impulsivity, recklessness and are more susceptible to peer pressure. They are inherently less responsible—which does not mean entirely un-responsible! Neuroscientists have shown that brain regions and systems responsible for foresight, self-regulation, risk assessment, responsiveness to social influences continue to mature until early adulthood.

Minors need to be considered differently than adults in sentencing due to differences in brain development, emotional maturity and their greater capacity for rehabilitation. As Alison Parker, Deputy Director of the U.S. Program at Human Rights Watch has put it: "Children are different than adults. They need to be punished for serious crimes but the punishment they receive needs to acknowledge their capacity for rehabilitation and life without parole does not do that."

Paradoxically, prisoners sentenced as juveniles to life-sentence without parole are actually less eligible for rehabilitation programs, for limited spaces in GED [General Educational Development] programs, substance abuse programs etc. A Human Rights Watch survey of California prisoners sentenced to life without parole as juveniles and, at 18, sent to maximum security prisons, found 59% reported having undergone physical or sexual assault. Nearly half of those surveyed said that they could not attend various educational or rehabilitation programs offered in prison. They have a lower priority for inclusion in limited-space programs than prisoners who are eligible, eventually, for parole.

You have nothing to gain, nothing to lose. You are given absolutely no incentive to improve yourself as a person.

One such prisoner told Human Rights Watch interviewers: "It makes you feel that life is not worth living because nothing you do, good or bad, matters to anyone. You have nothing to gain, nothing to lose. You are given absolutely no incentive to improve yourself as a person. It is hopeless." Without much doubt, many of the adolescents sentenced to life without parole have in common disturbing prior failures of their families, police, family courts, child protection agencies, foster-systems and health care providers to treat and protect them.

It Is Impossible to Know If a Juvenile Is Redeemable

The Florida judge who sentenced 16 year old Terrance Graham to life-sentence without parole claimed that the youth was simply unredeemable, beyond rehabilitation or deterrence and, thus, incapacitation was the only option. Lawyers and criminologists have argued, however, that it is very difficult, if not impossible, in the case of juveniles, to discriminate between those who can turn their lives around and those who are, perhaps, not really open to treatment. As the US bishops noted in their thoughtful 2000 Pastoral Letter, *Responsibility, Rehabilitation, Restoration*: "Not all offenders are open to treatment but all deserve to be challenged to turn their lives around." In that same letter, the bishops noted a larger issue of failures in our penal system: "The status quo is not really working—victims are often ignored, offenders are often not rehabilitated. Many communities have lost their sense of security". I was mindful of these failures as I prayed last week for a recent inmate at San Quentin Prison who hung himself his first day of incarceration. The Catholic chaplain asked our prayers for not only the young man but the failed system of prisons.

If I were going to make a prediction about the present case before the Supreme Court, I would predict a narrow 5-4 decision in favor of the Florida petitioners, although the Court has been chary about overturning state sentences not involving homicide. But even if the Court decides it is, technically, still constitutional, it remains inhumane and, in Catholic social thought, immoral.

5

Incarcerated Juveniles Are Often Abused and Mistreated

Julia Dahl

Julia Dahl is a contributing editor for the Crime Report.

Despite the $5 billion a year spent in the United States on juvenile corrections, many criminologists still argue that the system is in dire need of reform. Because the system does not invest the effort and money into rehabilitating these youth, more than half go on to commit crimes as adults. Not only do most juvenile detention centers not employ any type of counselor, but many are also caught up in scandals involving sexual and physical abuse. The key to keeping juveniles out of the justice system is to implement early intervention programs.

The U.S. spends $5 billion a year on juvenile corrections, but it's hard to argue that taxpayers are getting what they paid for. Many criminologists already agree that the country's criminal justice system is overdue for reform; but no area seems more in need of urgent attention than juvenile justice.

Statistics suggest that the huge investment is failing those most in need of help. In New York State, for example, a longitudinal study beginning in the early 1990s found that 85 percent of boys and 65 percent of girls who are incarcerated go on to be convicted of a felony as adults, according to Gladys Carrión, Commissioner of New York State's Office of Children and Family Services. Seventy percent of adult prisoners in California were once in foster care.

Julia Dahl, "Throw-Away Children: Juvenile Justice in Collapse," *The Crime Report*, February 9, 2010. Reproduced by permission.

According to Carrión, the system allows these young people to be treated like "throw-aways." "We obviously don't value them," she charges. "We incarcerate them and these are their lives' future outcomes."

Juvenile detention centers around the nation have been hit by a succession of scandals involving sexual and other types of physical abuse.

Moreover, although Carrión says that nearly 75 percent of incarcerated youth aged 10 to 17 have a diagnosable mental illness, most juvenile facilities have no on-staff counselors. And, if anything, today's juvenile justice system perpetuates an ugly cycle of crime and racial inequity: as of 2007, 1.7 million American children had a parent in prison, according to a report last year [2009] by the Sentencing Project. In 2008, arrest rates for robbery were 10 times higher for black youth than white, according to National Criminal Justice Reference Service figures cited by the Office of Juvenile Justice and Delinquent Protection.

Problems Begin Immediately

The problems are exacerbated from the moment a juvenile is caught up in the system. Juvenile detention centers around the nation have been hit by a succession of scandals involving sexual and other types of physical abuse.

"We are in the midst of a national crisis of abuse," says Barry Krisberg, a long-time youth advocate and distinguished senior fellow with the National Council on Crime and Delinquency.

Krisberg, who spoke at last week's [February 2010] John Jay/H.F. Guggenheim Conference on Crime in America, cited a recent Department of Justice study that found 12 percent of incarcerated youth report having been sexually abused. "It's a complete collapse of care," he said. "In these facilities young women are given dirty and torn underwear. The place smells bad. There's a fundamental breakdown of humanity that's allowed to go on."

Carrión, one of the country's most controversial juvenile justice figures, argues for fundamental reform of the system from the inside. She has used recent media exposés about the horrors of detention in her state's Tryon Residential Facility to push for closing such facilities and transforming their mission, as she puts it, from a "punitive model based on an adult correctional approach" to a more "therapeutic framework of young development."

She admits that it won't be easy. Conceding that Tryon and similar facilities lack in-house mental health workers even though nearly three-quarters of the state's incarcerated youth have mental illnesses, she observes there are few professionals willing to work with incarcerated youth for the meager state wage.

Unless young children in troubled circumstances get skilled and empathetic attention, their lives will go tragically off course.

Indeed. A blockbuster December 2009 report concluded that New York's juvenile prison system was so "broken" that Carrión's agency recommended New York State judges not to send *any* youths to detention centers unless they pose a significant public safety risk.

Krisberg, whom Carrión hired as a consultant, said that the state essentially gets what it pays for when it comes to corrections personnel, linking low wages and inadequate training directly to the problem. "In many cases, if a Kmart opens up, Kmart pays more than [the officers] are getting paid," he said. And without proper training to deal effectively with the psychological damage and subsequent bad behavior exhibited by most of the children, "staff are going to do what comes natural and oftentimes what comes natural is abusive."

Lack of Empathy Contributes to Problem

But, according to Krisberg, abuse is not the only problem inside juvenile facilities. He points to a lack of common sense and empathy by administrators. Krisberg related an experience he'd had in California where a black teenage girl was brought before a detention center disciplinary panel made up entirely of middle-aged white men and asked to describe her history of sexual abuse and molestation.

Not surprisingly, she felt unsafe relating such intimate, painful details before an audience of strangers she felt no connection with. So she stayed silent—and was given an extra 90 days on her time for failing to participate in her treatment.

Krisberg was floored: "They never thought, maybe we ought to get someone who knows something about young women, their development, their issues."

Most experts agree that by the time a young person enters the juvenile justice system, the system has already failed her. Unless young children in troubled circumstances get skilled and empathetic attention, their lives will go tragically off course.

Early Intervention Is the Key

Tony DiVittorio, creator of the Youth Guidance Becoming a Man (BAM) program in Chicago, works to prevent at-risk youth from getting caught up in the juvenile justice system by catching young men as soon as they exhibit disturbing behavior in school. BAM aims to help them learn personal responsibility, character development, and how to express their anger in normal and constructive ways. DiVittorio—whose 10-year-old program has expanded to 15 Chicago-area schools and is the subject of a University of Chicago study—says male mentoring is especially important in communities where father-son relationships are often strained or non-existent.

"It's all about prevention," he said at a special H.F. Guggenheim conference panel on juvenile justice last week [February 2010]. "If Michael's been referred to me because he's talking in class and getting suspensions and I say, 'I'm a counselor, why are you getting suspensions, what's your problem?' he shuts me out. [So instead] I say, 'what is it you want to say?' (and assure him) 'you have a lot to say.'"

Early intervention programs, which identify at-risk youngsters as early as two years old or younger, are also critical, says Sherry M. Cleary, Executive Director of New York City's Early Childhood Professional Development Institute. At the symposium, she offered a seemingly simple solution to help the youngest kids who are showing signs of acting up at primary school levels.

Food.

According to Cleary, providing kids with the right sustenance can go a long way toward keeping them out of contact with the criminal justice system.

"Thirty-five years ago I had food in my classroom, because when children came in they were starving and they couldn't pay attention," she said. "When you're hungry, you're crabby, and when you're crabby you hit people. So do you want to criminalize that child or do you feed them?"

6

Opponents of Juvenile LWOP Misrepresent the Facts

Charles D. Stimson

Charles D. Stimson is senior legal fellow at The Heritage Foundation's Center for Legal and Judicial Studies.

For several years now, lawmakers and activists have been attempting to do away with sentences of life without parole (LWOP) for juveniles. Fortunately, these attempts have been unsuccessful. Media coverage of this debate has been one-sided in favor of opponents of LWOP and has propagated misleading and sometimes incorrect information. The opponents of juvenile LWOP are well funded and know how to manipulate their resources and information to benefit their cause. Factual information must be available to encourage and foster informed debate.

[The August 2009 Heritage Foundation report "Adult Time for Adult Crimes: Life Without Parole for Juvenile Killers and Violent Teens"] was undertaken in response to litigation and legislation against the use of life-without-parole [LWOP] sentences for juvenile offenders. Following several challenges in state supreme courts, interest in the issue has only grown since the U.S. Supreme Court agreed to hear two cases challenging life-without-parole-sentences for juvenile offenders on Eighth Amendment grounds. Recent years have also witnessed the introduction, in several states, of legislation prohibiting the practice. California's experience with such legislation is typical.

Charles D. Stimson, "Adult Time for Adult Crime: Sentencing Under Siege," *The Foundry*, October 19, 2009. Reproduced by permission.

In 2007, State Senator Leland Yee introduced a bill to radically alter the sentence of life without parole for juvenile offenders in California. Specifically, Senate Bill No. 999 would have ended the use of these sentences prospectively. Under the legislation, any juvenile offender convicted of first-degree murder, with any number of aggravating circumstances (such as multiple murders, murder for hire, murder of a police officer or firefighter, and torture of the victim), would be punishable by, at most, a life sentence with the possibility of parole after 25 years.

The debate over the measure was conducted largely by national special-interest groups. On one side were a variety of activist groups that have engaged on this issue in a number of states, including the American Civil Liberties Union (ACLU), Human Rights Watch (HRW), Amnesty International (AI), Equal Justice Initiative, and NAACP [National Association for the Advancement of Colored People] Legal Defense and Educational Fund. On the other side, opposing the legislation, were local groups representing prosecutors, police, and victims. These opponents ultimately proved successful, and the bill died at the conclusion of the legislative session.

In February 2009, with the support of the same activist groups, Senator Yee introduced an even more radical proposal than Senate Bill No. 999. Without banning life-without-parole sentences for juveniles, Senate Bill No. 399 would allow any prisoner who has served 10 to 15 years of a life-without-parole sentence for an offense committed when he or she was less than 18 years old to petition the sentencing court for "recall" (i.e., cancellation) of the existing sentence, a rehearing, and a new, reduced sentence. The court would then choose whether to accept the petition.

The Safety of the Community Is at Risk

The court would have no such choice, however, if the prisoner satisfies three of eight criteria, including whether the prisoner had an adult codefendant; has "maintained family ties" while in prison; has not maintained ties with criminals outside of prison; suffered from "cognitive limitations" at the time of the offense (perhaps even being a juvenile); has taken a class while in prison; used self-study while in prison; and has taken some "action that demonstrates the presence of remorse." Notably, whether the prisoner would present a danger to the community is not among the criteria.

With these easily satisfied criteria, practically every prisoner sentenced to life without parole for an offense committed while a juvenile would be entitled to recall and a resentencing hearing. Under this system, individuals sentenced to life without parole could actually be released from prison before those sentenced to lesser terms for less serious or less heinous offenses.

News coverage of the 2007 and 2009 measures [to do away with LWOP for juveniles] has generally been one-sided.

After quick initial progress, the 2009 legislation met the same fate as its predecessor. The bill cleared the California Senate in early June, having passed through two committees with little opposition, before going down to a quick and unexpected defeat at the end of the month in the Assembly's Committee on Public Safety.

Media Coverage One-Sided and Misleading

News coverage of the 2007 and 2009 measures has generally been one-sided, with reporters quoting the sponsor of the bills and activist supporters. More troubling are the unsupported assertions made by supporters, including that "children" should never face severe adult sentences, that [the 2005 Supreme Court case *Roper v. Simmons*, which held it unconstitutional to issue the death penalty for crimes committed while under the age of eighteen] ... cast doubt on the constitutionality of life without parole for juvenile offenders, that ending such sentences would significantly reduce prison overcrowding, and that many who were serving such sentences were mere accomplices to or observers of the crimes with which they were charged.

Further, the sponsor's statement in the bills' official analyses contained highly questionable assertions of fact. For example, the statement for the current version of the bill claims that "59% of youth sentenced to LWOP are first-time offenders" and that "45% of the youth sentenced to life in prison did not perform the murder they were convicted of." It provides no sources for or explanation of these claims. It also states that "70% of the youth acted under the influence of adults" and that, "in 56% of these cases, the youth received a higher sentence than the adults."

The bill further claims that "[t]he U.S. is the only country in the world that sentences kids to life without parole." This is simply false. As even Amnesty International and Human Rights Watch acknowledge, at least 11 other countries allow life without parole for juvenile offenders, and the true number is likely greater, as explained below. The bill's sponsor and supporters have made many other claims that do not stand up to even light scrutiny. Our skepticism in the face of these assertions led us to research these claims. The leading sources on life without parole for juvenile offenders, and frequently the only sources consulted by those with an interest in the issue, were one-sided reports by many of the same activist groups that had supported the California legislation. This was, we learned, no accident.

Opponents Manipulate Their Resources

Opponents of tough sentences for serious juvenile offenders have been working for years to abolish the sentence of life without the possibility of parole. Though representing relatively few, these groups are highly organized, well-funded, and passionate about their cause. Emboldened by the Supreme Court's decision in *Roper*, which relied on the "cruel and unusual punishments" language of the Eighth Amendment to the Constitution to prohibit capital sentences for juveniles, they have set about to extend the result of *Roper* to life without parole.

These groups wrap their reports and other products in the language of *Roper* and employ sympathetic terms like "child" and "children" and *Roper*-like language such as "death sentence" instead of the actual sentence of life without parole. Their reports are adorned with pictures of children, most of whom appear to be five to eight years old, despite the fact that the youngest person serving life without parole in the United States is 14 years old and most are 17 or 18 years old.

The problem is that this important public policy debate has been shaped by a carefully crafted campaign of misinformation.

A careful reading of these groups' reports, articles, and press releases reveals that their messages and themes have been tightly coordinated. There is a very unsubtle similarity in terminology among organizations in characterizing the sentence of life without parole for juvenile offenders. For example, they consistently decline to label teenage offenders "juveniles" despite the fact that the term is used by the states, lawyers, prosecutors, state statutes, judges, parole officers, and everyone else in the juvenile justice system. Instead, they use "child."

There is nothing wrong, of course, with advocacy groups coordinating their language and message. The problem is that this important public policy debate has been shaped by a carefully crafted campaign of misinformation.

The issue of juvenile offenders and the proper sentence they are due is much too important to be driven by manufactured statistics, a misreading of a Supreme Court case, and fallacious assertions that the United States is in violation of international law. Instead, the debate should be based on real facts and statistics, a proper reading of precedent, an intelligent understanding of federal and state sovereignty, and a proper understanding of our actual international obligations.

The Public Misled by One-Sided Debate

Regrettably, that has not been the case, as opponents of life without parole for juvenile offenders have monopolized the debate. As a result, legislatures, courts, the media, and the public have been misled on crucial points.

Nearly every report contains sympathetic summaries of juvenile offenders' cases that gloss over the real facts of the crimes.

One prominent example is a frequently cited statistic on the number of juvenile offenders currently serving life-without-parole sentences. Nearly all reports published on the subject and dozens of newscasts and articles based on those reports state that there are at least 2,225 juveniles sentenced to life without parole. That number first appeared in a 2005 report by Amnesty International and Human Rights Watch, "The Rest of Their Lives: Life Without Parole for Child Offenders in the United States."

But a careful look at the data and consultation with primary sources—that is, state criminal-justice officials—reveals that this statistic is seriously flawed. As described below, officials in some states reject as incorrect the figures assigned to their states. Others admit that they have no way of knowing how many juvenile offenders in their states have been sentenced to life without parole—and that, by extension, neither could activist groups.

Nonetheless, this statistic has gone unchallenged even as it has been cited in appellate briefs and oral arguments before state supreme courts and even in a petition to the United States Supreme Court. All of these courts have been asked to make public policy based on factual representations that even cursory research would demonstrate are questionable.

Another example is the unrealistic portrait of the juvenile offenders who are sentenced to life without parole that activist groups have painted. Nearly every report contains sympathetic summaries of juvenile offenders' cases that gloss over the real facts of the crimes, deploying lawyerly language and euphemism to disguise brutality and violence.

For example, consider the case of Ashley Jones. The Equal Justice Initiative's 2007 report describes Ms. Jones's offense as follows: "At 14, Ashley tried to escape the violence and abuse by running away with an older boyfriend who shot and killed her grandfather and aunt. Her grandmother and sister, who were injured during the offense, want Ashley to come home."

The judge's account of the facts, however, presents a somewhat different picture. An excerpt:

> When Ashley realized her aunt was still breathing, she hit her in the head with a heater, stabbed her in the chest and attempted to set her room on fire. . . . As ten-year old Mary Jones [Ashley's sister] attempted to run, Ashley grabbed her and began hitting her. [Ashley's boyfriend] put the gun in young Mary's face and told her that that was how she would die. Ashley intervened and said, "No, let me do it," and proceeded to stab her little sister fourteen times.

In a similar vein, many of the studies feature pictures of children who are far younger than any person actually serving life without parole in the United States. When these reports do include an actual picture of a juvenile offender, the picture is often one taken years before the crime was committed. The

41

public could be forgiven for believing incorrectly that children under 14 are regularly sentenced to life behind bars without the possibility of release.

A final example is the legality of life-without-parole sentences for juvenile offenders. Opponents make the claim, among many others, that these sentences violate the United States' obligations under international law. Yet they usually fail to mention that no court has endorsed this view, and rarely do they explain the implications of the fact that the United States has not ratified the treaty that they most often cite, the Convention on the Rights of the Child, and has carved out legal exceptions (called "reservations") to others.

Further, they often abuse judicial precedent by improperly extending the death penalty—specific logic and language of *Roper* into the non-death penalty arena, an approach that the Supreme Court has repeatedly rejected. Again, the public could be forgiven for believing incorrectly that the Supreme Court, particularly in *Roper*, has all but declared the imposition of life sentences without parole for juvenile offenders to be unconstitutional. A more honest reading of the precedent, however, compels the opposite conclusion: that the sentence is not constitutionally suspect.

Presenting the Whole Story

Public policy should be based on facts, not false statistics and misleading legal claims. For that reason, we undertook the research to identify those states that have authorized life without parole for juvenile offenders and wrote to every major district attorney's office across those 43 states. To understand how prosecutors are using life-without-parole sentences and the types of crimes and criminals for which such sentences are imposed, we asked each office for case digests of juvenile offenders who were prosecuted by their offices and received the specific sentence of life without parole.

The response from prosecutors around the country was overwhelming. Prosecutors from across the United States sent us case digests, including official court documents, police reports, judges' findings, photos of the defendants and victims, motions, newspaper articles, and more. From that collection of case digests, we selected 16 typical cases, all concerning juvenile offenders, and assembled a complete record for each. Those cases are presented as studies in this report. In sharp contrast to the practices of other reports, these case studies recount all of the relevant facts of the crimes, as found by a jury or judge and recorded in official records (which are cited), in neutral language.

The text of the report itself includes a neutral analysis of the relevant case law and Supreme Court precedents, as well as an analysis of how international law affects domestic practice in this area. It also includes a rough analysis (which is all the present data will allow) of the statistics often used in activist groups' reports and a comparison of U.S. and international juvenile crime statistics.

To foster informed debate, more facts . . . are needed about the use of life-without-parole sentences for juvenile offenders.

Based on this research, we conclude that the sentence of life without parole for juvenile offenders is reasonable, constitutional, and (appropriately) rare. Our survey of the cases shows that some juveniles commit horrific crimes with full knowledge of their actions and intent to bring about the results. In constitutional terms, the Supreme Court's own jurisprudence, including *Roper*, draws a clear line between the sentence of death and all others, including life without parole; further, to reach its result, *Roper* actually depends on the availability of life without parole for juvenile offenders. We also find that while most states allow life-without-parole sentences for juvenile offenders, judges generally have broad discretion in sentencing, and most juvenile offenders do not receive that sentence.

We conclude, then, that reports by activist groups on life without parole for juvenile offenders are at best misleading and in some instances simply wrong in their facts, analyses, conclusions, and recommendations. Regrettably, the claims made by these groups have been repeated so frequently that lawmakers, judges, the media, and the public risk losing sight of their significant bias.

To foster informed debate, more facts—particularly, good state-level statistics—are needed about the use of life-without-parole sentences for juvenile offenders. But even on the basis of current data, as insufficient as they are, legislators should take note of how these sentences are actually applied and reject any attempts to repeal life-without-parole sentences for juvenile offenders.

Juvenile LWOP Offers Victims' Families Closure

Liza Matia

Liza Matia is a staff writer for the Clearfield, Pennsylvania, newspaper the Progress.

In a 2008 Pennsylvania public hearing to address juvenile life without parole (LWOP) and whether or not these sentences are too harsh, the families of eight victims were invited to take part in the debate and present their side of the story. Although these families presented their cases in graphic detail, reliving the horrific details, they felt that the hearing was very one-sided, with many more opponents of juvenile life without parole than proponents. While this was only a hearing to discuss the fairness of these sentences, many victims and their families believe that the possibility for the sentences to change unfairly forces them to relive the crimes at regular parole hearings to see that justice continues to be served.

Is life without parole [LWOP] inhumane for juveniles who commit crimes? That's the question circulating in Harrisburg [Pennsylvania's capital] and around the state.

In September [2008], Jodi Dotts and Ron Klotz, two local parents of murdered children, along with advocates from the Clearfield County Victim Witness Office, attended a public informational hearing at the Capitol.

Liza Matia, "Parents Fight to Keep Juvenile Killers in Prison," *The Progress*, Clearfield, PA. November 22, 2008. Reproduced by permission.

Determining the Fairness of Juvenile LWOP

The purpose of the hearing, led by Sen. Stewart Greenleaf, (R-Montco-Bucks) was to hear arguments as to why Pennsylvania leads the nation in the highest number of juveniles sentenced to life without parole and whether or not their life sentences should be reformed. Sen. Greenleaf wanted to make sure that no injustice was being done and that the state's system was operating fairly.

Watchdog groups like Human Rights Watch are urging states to abolish life sentences without parole for juveniles and to do so retroactively.

According to Clearfield County District Attorney William A. Shaw Jr., "This is an attempt to change the law regarding murder. The law already takes into consideration the age of offenders. In many situations, it is an issue for the jury to decide if the offender should be convicted of murder in the first degree or if circumstances justify a conviction to a lesser degree of murder."

When Judy Shirey, coordinator of the Clearfield County Victim Witness office, first received notification about the hearing, she "got all fired up."

"It hits you," she said. At first, she wasn't sure if the hearing could relate to any Clearfield County cases, but she would soon learn that two local cases would qualify.

Two Cases That Would Be Affected

Andrew Callahan and Jessica Holtmeyer were both teens when they were sentenced to life without the possibility of parole after being convicted of first-degree murder. In 1997, Mr. Callahan shot and killed his 16-year-old classmate, Micah Pollock, and dumped his body in a beaver dam in the Pine Run area. He was convicted in 1998 and again in 2007 when he was retried for the murder. Ms. Holtmeyer was convicted in 1998 for the hanging death of 15-year-old Kimberly Jo Dotts in a rural area of Bradford Township. Six other teens were involved in the case.

Ms. Shirey alerted Mr. Klotz, Micah's father, and Ms. Dotts, the mother of Kimberly, that notification of the hearing was on the way.

"We handled it together," Ms. Shirey said.

Ms. Dotts described the letter as "the scariest letter ever," but both she and Mr. Klotz knew that they "had to be part of this."

Ms. Shirey contacted the Office of the Victim Advocate in Harrisburg and described each case in graphic detail. In order to hear both sides of the story at the hearing, the Senate Judiciary Committee invited testimony of the victims from the eligible cases. Both Ms. Dotts and Mr. Klotz were chosen to testify. They were two of only eight victims who would present their sides of the story.

Ms. Dotts said she was "so excited to be picked" and wanted people to know what Ms. Holtmeyer and Mr. Callahan did. She felt it was important for them to hear her feelings and emotions during the testimony.

"This was one of the hardest things we've ever had to sit through and hear," Ms. Dotts said of the hearing. She described listening to testimony from inmates who were convicted as juveniles and sentenced to life in prison. She said the inmates talked about being rehabilitated and deserving second chances at life.

"But my daughter, his son," she said, motioning to Mr. Klotz, "weren't given a second chance."

The hearing also featured testimony from church groups, watchdog groups and church leaders who felt that life sentences for juveniles was inhumane. Ms. Dotts said that one woman argued that the human brain isn't fully developed until age 30.

"These kids knew right from wrong," Ms. Dotts said of the inmates who testified. "They made the decision."

Despite their stories of rehabilitation, what struck Ms. Dotts most about the inmates' testimony was their lack of remorse.

"They never said they were ever sorry for what they did," she said. "It was all about 'me' and second chances."

She said that she and Mr. Klotz held up photos of Micah and Kimberly because they wanted people to see how young their children were when they were murdered.

While the inmates expressed no remorse, Ms. Dotts also said she had difficulty feeling sorry for them. She said she doesn't feel that criminals, like Ms. Holtmeyer, are being treated inhumanely because she learned they have access to the Internet and are provided with the basic needs like food, clothing and shelter.

The Hearing Felt Very One-Sided

The two described the hearing as a "hostile environment" and felt that everyone was against them.

"We were like defendants," Mr. Klotz said.

The victims felt that there was an imbalance in attendance because there seemed to be more proponents for abolishing the life sentence than those who were against it. Some even left while victims were testifying.

The only salvation that parents ... have is knowing that their children's murderers are locked up.

"They didn't want to hear us," Ms. Dotts said. "They only wanted to hear one side."

Mr. Klotz pointed out that in order for juveniles to qualify for the charge of first-degree murder, they had to have murdered or been an accessory to a murder.

"That's not the mind of a child," he said.

According to Ms. Dotts, the only salvation that parents like she and Mr. Klotz have is knowing that their children's murderers are locked up.

The Nightmare Is Never Over

"But every year, I know there's the chance for appeals," she said. Ms. Dotts said that the part of "life without parole" is the "only thing we have to hold on to."

If advocacy groups get their way, there could be nothing left for victims like Ms. Dotts and Mr. Klotz to hold onto.

"A change in the law would be devastating to victims," Mr. Shaw said. "In PA, life without parole means life without parole, and it is unfair to make victims now worry that a previously convicted offender may now be considered for parole."

According to Ms. Shirey, if the sentence of life without parole is abolished, the inmates will appear before the state parole board, and will eventually be released.

Ms. Dotts said that she pleaded with the parole board not to release one of the girls involved in her daughter's murder, but they did.

"I did everything I could do," she said. "It's never over. There's never any closure."

Ms. Shirey noted that while the hearing they attended was just that and no action was taken, "the door is open" for something more to happen.

"Just because the hearing's over doesn't mean it will stop," Mr. Klotz said.

In the cases of Ms. Holtmeyer and Mr. Callahan, Ms. Shirey said that the cases could be revisited and the sentences reworded.

"Our juveniles are on that list. We worry about that," Ms. Dotts said. "Our voices need to be heard. We need to be taken seriously."

8

Some Victims' Families Oppose Juvenile LWOP

Linda L. White

Linda L. White is a member of Murder Victims' Families for Reconciliation and has acted as an adjunct faculty member at Sam Houston State University where she taught courses in psychology, philosophy, and criminal justice.

Contrary to what the proponents of juvenile life without parole (LWOP) would have the public believe, not all victims and their families support this sentence. There are some that take a more productive route, seeking education and understanding and eventually come to forgive the perpetrator. After coming to know the juveniles that committed the crime against them or their loved ones, they come to understand how a young person may come to travel down such a path. They also begin to feel that giving up on the young person and locking them up with no chance of parole is not as productive as realizing that they are, in fact, only children and need to be treated as such. This includes holding them accountable for their crimes, but also giving them the chance to reform themselves and develop into productive members of society.

Until November of 1986, I was not very knowledgeable or very interested, to be quite frank, in criminal justice matters in general, and certainly not juvenile justice matters. That changed quite suddenly and dramatically late that November

Linda L. White, "Issue: Juvenile Life Without the Possibility of Parole," Testimony Before the US House of Representatives, Committee on the Judiciary, Washington, D.C., June 9, 2009.

when our 26-year-old daughter Cathy went missing for five days and was then found dead following a sexual assault by two 15-year-old boys. I spent the better part of a year in limbo awaiting their trials, as they had both been certified to stand trial as adults.

During that time, the only information I had on either of them was that they both had long juvenile records. There was never any doubt about their guilt, as they had confessed to the rape and murder and led the police to her body after they had been detained by the police in another city in Texas. The court-appointed attorneys for both pled them out and they were sentenced to long prison terms with no chance at parole for at least eighteen years. They came up for parole in 2004 and were both given five year set-offs, so they remain in prison at this time. I assume they will come up again later on this year [2009].

Punishment is the least effective means to change behavior.

Gaining Understanding Through Education

The year after my daughter was murdered, I returned to college to become a death educator and grief counselor. Since that time, I have received a bachelor's degree in psychology, a master's degree in clinical psychology, and a doctorate in educational human resource development with a focus in adult education. I fell in love with teaching along the way and never got my professional counseling credentials, but I have counseled informally through church and my teaching. During the time I taught at the university level, I taught upper level college courses for eight and a half years in prison, the most rewarding work I have ever done, and the most healing for me as the mother of a murder victim.

In addition to the formal schooling I've had, I have also educated myself in the area of criminal justice. I heard a lot of information when I attended victims' groups and I wanted to know if it was accurate. I have found out that, for the most part, it was not. One notable example: Texas prisons are about as far as you can get from country clubs. Many of our citizens, and certainly victims of crime, want the men and women who are convicted of criminal activity to suffer as much as possible in prison, believing that this is the way they will turn from a life of crime. I no longer believe this to be true, and I have become a devout believer in restorative justice as opposed to retributive justice. It does not mean that I think incarceration is always wrong, but neither do I believe that it should be our first inclination, for juveniles or for adults. And neither am I a great believer in long sentences, for most offenders. As a psychology student and teacher, I have learned that punishment is the least effective means to change behavior, and that it often has negative side-effects as well.

Focusing on Healing the Family

My journey to healing after my daughter's murder was different than what I often see in victim/survivors, for I had concentrated on healing for my family and me, and because I focused on education over the years. At first it was education about grief and how to help my young granddaughter with hers, and then, when I returned to college, it became about psychology and issues related to death and dying. Eventually, it became concentrated in criminal justice. Early on I saw much that was violent in our system perhaps necessarily so at times—but still, it seemed to me that we returned violence for violence in so many ways. I kept my mind and heart open to another means of doing justice, one that would be based on non-violent ideals and means. Restorative justice is that paradigm and I have become one of its greatest proponents. That is what actually led me to seek a mediated conversation with either of the young men who killed my Cathy.

As I said previously, for many years, I only knew that the boys who killed my daughter were juveniles with long criminal records. In 2000, I found out that one of them, Gary Brown, was willing to meet with me in a mediated dialogue as part of a program that we have in our Texas Department of Criminal Justice's Victims' Services Division. He was apparently very remorseful by that time and had prayed for a chance to tell us that. During the next year, Gary, with the help of our mediator Ellen Halbert, and my daughter Ami (Cathy's daughter whom we had raised and adopted) and I did a great deal of reflective work to prepare for our meeting. During that time I found out from Gary's records that his long juvenile record began at the age of eight with his running away from abusive situations, both at home and in foster care eventually. If I were being abused emotionally, physically, and sexually, I think I'd run away, too; it seems quite rational to me. I also found out that his first suicide attempt was at the age of eight, the first of ten attempts. I have a grandson just about that age right now, and it breaks my heart to think of a child like that trying to take his own life because it is so miserable.

Until the time that I met with Gary, I had never laid eyes on him and had, over the years, gradually come to ignore his existence. Both the offenders became non-persons to me, in effect. Once I knew that Gary wanted to meet me, that nonpersonhood totally changed for me; he became as human to me as the men I had taught in prison. That in and of itself was a relief, I think, since part of me revolted at the idea of forgetting him in any way at all. As the time approached for us to meet, I know that my daughter and Gary both became more and more apprehensive, but not me. I couldn't wait to see him and tell him how much I believed in his remorse and was grateful for it. I know that this unusual response to the killer of one's beloved child was only possible through my discovery of restorative justice and, of course, by the grace of

God. I strongly believe that most of my journey over the last 22 years had been through grace. Otherwise, I have no explanation for it.

Sentencing youth to life without parole strips our young people of hope and the opportunity for rehabilitation.

Using Experience to Help Other Victims

My meeting with him was everything I expected and more. Since it was made into a documentary, I have been privileged to have it shown around the world for training and educational purposes, and I have heard from many who have seen it and felt blessed by the experience. I am sometimes invited to go with the film to answer questions and reflect on my experience. I also go into prison, especially with a victim/offender encounter program we have in Texas called Bridges to Life, a faith-based restorative justice curriculum, where my film is used to educate offenders related to victim empathy. I have been deeply blessed by this work and I feel Cathy's presence in it every time I stand before a group either in or out of prison and reflect on my journey.

My education and years of teaching developmental psychology have taught me that young people are just different qualitatively from the adults we hope they become. And my experience with Gary has taught me that we have a responsibility to protect our youth from the kind of childhood that he had, and from treatment that recklessly disregards their inherent vulnerability as children. Sentencing youth to life without parole strips our young people of hope and the opportunity for rehabilitation. It ignores what science tells us: that youth are fundamentally different from adults both physically and emotionally. Even given the trauma, and incredible loss my family experienced, I still believe that young people need to be held accountable in a way that reflects their ability to grow and change. Gary is proof that young people, even those who have done horrible things, can be reformed.

9

Victims' Families Have Differing Opinions on Juvenile LWOP

Lisa Rea

Lisa Rea has an extensive background in restorative justice. She founded the Justice and Reconciliation Project, which organized victims of violent crime around criminal justice reform.

While many people may be in agreement on the subject of restorative justice, these same people may not be in agreement on the topic of juveniles being sentenced to life without parole (LWOP). Before any common ground can be found in this debate, both sides must develop a respect for each other. Once dialogue is established, both sides can work together to improve the broken criminal justice system

I would like to draw your attention to a very controversial piece of US federal legislation, HR 2289, which seeks to address the problem of juvenile lifers who are serving life sentences.

The expressed purpose of the bill is to "establish a meaningful opportunity for parole or similar release of juvenile offenders sentenced to life in prison."

Two victims of crime who have been active on many issues related to criminal justice reform testified at this hearing in June [2009] before the Senate Subcommittee on Crime,

Lisa Rea, "Violent Juveniles Serving Life Without Parole: When Victims of Crime Disagree," Restorative Justice Online, April 9, 2010. Reproduced by permission of the author.

Terrorism and Homeland Security in Washington, D.C. The witnesses included Linda White, member of Murder Victims for Reconciliation, from Texas and Jennifer Bishop-Jenkins, co-founder of the National Organization of Victims of Juvenile Lifers, from Illinois. Both victims were at one time working with my organization, The Justice and Reconciliation Project, a national nonprofit that organized and educated victims of crime about restorative justice. Until the closing of the JRP this year, Ms. Jenkins served on the board of directors of JRP. Both victims support restorative justice. Yet, on this subject they do not see eye to eye.

As you listen to the hearing, or read the testimony, you will hear restorative justice mentioned. The issue of how to treat juveniles offenders who have received life sentences without the possibility of parole is a very tough issue. This bill, HR 2289, called the Juvenile Justice Accountability and Improvement Act of 2009, is looking at how we sentence violent juveniles to life in prison and opening the debate about future treatment and sentencing of such violent juveniles. My hope is to stimulate discussion on this subject especially in the light of restorative justice. I hope that with this national discussion it might be possible to come to a place of common ground especially among the crime victims' community.

Bringing family members before a parole board every 2–3 years . . . has a devastating effect on the victim's family for life.

I am aware that Ms. Jenkins' concerns include the issue of retroactivity; that is, how to apply this type of legislation to cases where such juveniles have already received a life without parole sentence. This legislation as it is now written would re-open cases like Jennifer's. Jennifer's sister, Nancy Bishop Langert, her husband, Richard, and their un-born child were victims of a vicious murder in 1990. The life sentence that applies to the offender in her family's case would be in question. While the offender received a life without parole sentence, the chance of the offender getting out of prison some day has victims like Jennifer reeling. Part of Jennifer's argument is that bringing family members before a parole board every 2–3 years for the rest of their lives, given that family members often do oppose release of violent offenders after the murder of a loved one, has a devastating effect on the victim's family for life.

Linda White, also a victim of violent crime whose daughter Cathy was brutally murdered in 1986, sees it differently. Ms. White believes we should treat juvenile offenders differently, especially since the acts of violence committed by these juveniles were committed often at an early age. White also argues that through rehabilitation type programs change in an offender is possible. She believes that at the very least these juvenile offenders should have the chance for parole. White met the man who killed her daughter in a mediated dialogue set up through the Texas Department of Criminal Justice and its Victim's Services Division. This dialogue had a deep effect on Ms. White and her view of this offender.

Victims should always have the right to be at the table when laws are made that will affect them.

I will not go into every argument posed by each victim as they testified. You can view that for yourself. But it is clear to me that victims should always have the right to be at the table when laws are made that will affect them. In a system based on restorative justice that would be the ideal. That, after all, is what restorative justice is all about. I call it victims-driven restorative justice, for without the victim in the center all good reforms of the criminal justice are not restorative justice. Should the views of victims have more weight than others? I think the views of victims should carry weight, yes. How much weight they should wield is the question. Increasingly, though, crime victims are disagreeing publicly on many issues. Some of those issues include the death penalty, and whether it should be abolished, or whether we need additional laws that require offenders to serve more and more prison time (or even be eligible for the death penalty), or this issue considering whether juveniles should be given life without parole sentences.

Brokering a position on legislation, no matter how complicated, is something that happens all the time. I know because I've written legislation and have lobbied for and against legislation related to many subjects, including issues related to criminal justice. This is not new. Can common ground be built? I think it can even on this highly explosive subject. But it will take some kind of give and take on both sides. One thing is essential, however. There must be mutual respect between the two (or more) sides as the negotiations on the legislation takes place. Certainly this legislation will not stand or fall because of the views of crime victims; however, saying that, it is also my experience that their views do matter and lawmakers do listen. Public opinion is also affected by the stories they hear from crime victims.

Isn't that what restorative justice is all about? A dialogue must begin. What are we trying to fix here? I would say we are trying to fix a terribly broken criminal justice system that does not work for the victim (or their families), the offender (and yes, their families) and the communities torn by crime. How do we move past this to a place of safer communities that begin to restore or heal victims as much as possible as well as the communities also in need of restoration? We sit down and have that dialogue.

10

The Legal System Is Harder on Juveniles than on Adults

Liliana Segura

Liliana Segura is a staff writer and the editor of Rights and Liberties and World Special Coverage for the online newsmagazine AlterNet.

Juveniles sentenced to life without parole are often caught up in crimes perpetrated by older teens or adults. With the crimes being pinned on the juvenile, they often get tougher sentences than others involved in the crime. But some experts argue that many of the youths that are locked up have the potential to become productive members of society.

Sara Kruzan was 11 years old, a middle school student from Riverside, Calif., when she met a man—he called himself GG—who was almost three times her age. GG took her under his wing; he would buy her gifts, take her and her friends rollerskating. "He was like a father figure," she recalls.

Despite suffering severe bouts of depression as a child, until then, Kruzan was a good student, an "overachiever" in her words. But her mother was abusive and addicted to drugs; as for her father, she had only met him a couple of times. So, more and more, GG filled in.

"GG was there—sometimes," she said. "He would talk to me and take me out and give me all these lavish gifts and do all these things for me. . . ." Before long, he started talking to

Liliana Segura, "16-Year Old Got Life Without Parole for Killing Her Abusive Pimp—Should Teens Be Condemned to Die in Jail?" *AlterNet*, October 31, 2009. Reproduced by permission.

Factoring in Race

Another major factor is race. During Sullivan's trial, "the prosecutor and witnesses made repeated, unnecessary reference to the fact that Joe is African American and the victim (was) white," according to EJI. "One witness repeatedly said the perpetrator of the assault was a 'colored boy' or 'a dark colored boy.'"

It is not news that the American criminal justice system disproportionately targets people of color. But when it comes to juvenile offenders, Alison Parker calls the disparities "absolutely shocking." On a national level, "African American youth are serving the sentence at a rate of about 10 times that of white youth," Parker told *AlterNet*. "In some states, the rate is even higher."

In both cases before the Supreme Court, the defendants were sentenced to life for crimes that fell short of murder, a phenomenon that is especially prevalent in Florida, where the number of prisoners who will die in jail for non-homicide crimes hovers at 77.

Terrance Jamar Graham, the defendant in *Graham v. Florida*, was 17 years old and on probation for a crime he committed when he was 16, when he took part in an armed burglary. His co-defendants got minor sentences. He was slapped with life without parole.

"Mr. Graham, as I look back on your case, yours is really candidly a sad situation," the judge told him. "The only thing that I can rationalize is that you decided that this is how you were going to lead your life and there is nothing that we can do for you."

This is classic "three strikes" logic, which, along with the conspiracy and felony murder statutes, have led teens to be sentenced to life for crimes in which they played only a minor role.

Take Christine Lockhart, the first female juvenile to be sentenced to life without parole in Iowa. She was 17 years old and sitting in a car when her boyfriend killed someone during an armed robbery. Today, she has been in prison for more than half her life.

Lockhart, along with Sara Kruzan are a relative minority, two out of some 175 women serving life without parole for crimes they committed as teenagers. But their stories reveal how young people can get caught up in dangerous, harmful, and ultimately deadly, situations often simply by being with the wrong people at the wrong time.

"Sara's story is compelling," says Parker. "But it is really one that is shared across the country. There are many, many people with similar circumstances who are serving life sentences without any possibility of parole."

Finally Getting Some Help

Kruzan, in fact, is one of the lucky ones. She now has attorneys who are working on appealing her sentence, pro bono. Most other prisoners serving life without parole for crimes committed as juveniles have no post-conviction representation at all.

Today, Kruzan is 32 years old and described as a "model inmate," despite any real lack of incentive. ("Who wants to excel in prison?" she says.) Asked what she would say if she had a chance to appear before a a parole board, she says that she believes she can now be of some value to society, perhaps even a "positive example."

Also, she says, "I've learned what moral scruples are."

11

The Justice System Is Prejudiced Against Juveniles of Color

James Bell

James Bell is the founder and the executive director of the W. Haywood Burns Institute, a nonprofit organization fighting for equality and ethical treatment in the juvenile justice field.

There are many factors and statistics used in the arguments for and against juvenile sentences of life without parole (LWOP); however, the statistics involving the much higher percentage of blacks serving life sentences than whites are very rarely mentioned. This has even spread to elementary schools and their "zero tolerance" policies. Not only do the children suffer, but society pays the price as well, morally and financially. As a society, we should expect better of our policy makers and the juvenile justice system.

I continue to be amazed at how many people continue to behave as though race and involvement with the criminal justice system are synonymous. Has it become an accepted fact of life in the United States that the machinery of justice applies almost solely to people of color? I shuddered to realize this once again while reading editorials about the Supreme Court's deliberations regarding juveniles receiving life imprisonment without the possibility of parole [LWOP] in the U.S., the only country that engages in this barbaric practice.

An Overlooked Fact About Juvenile LWOP

While I was heartened by the arguments proffered regarding brain development and laws that restrict children from voting, serving on juries, buying alcohol and cigarettes—something was missing. In most of the editorials in mainstream media, it was rare to find any analysis of race and how justice systems operate in neighborhoods made up mostly of people of color in poverty. In the alternative press, an *AlterNet* article mentioned an important fact: Black prisoners account for 84 percent of those in prison for life without the possibility of parole in Florida, the state with the most people expected to perish this way in prison. Nationally, black youths are serving life without parole at a rate of about 10 times that of white youths, according to Human Rights Watch. Amy Bach's recent book, *Ordinary Injustice: How America Holds Court*, further recounts such justice by geography and race.

As someone who works every day to prevent youth of color from being undeservedly trapped by the labyrinth that is today's justice system, perplexed is an understatement to describe my feelings as reporters and commentators continue to accept the disproportionate impact of justice on communities of color. We must combat the normalization of this phenomenon. Why isn't it a story that most black and brown youth are detained for low-level administrative violations rather than crimes that endanger public safety? Why isn't there more media attention around the fact that youth of color are securely confined in numbers that cannot be accounted for by crime alone? Why is there not more scrutiny regarding biased decision-making that when examined with data shows that for the same offenses for which white youth are released, youth of color are detained?

An Example of the Race Issue

These are tough questions to answer when one realizes that at the heart of such issues is yet another conversation about race.

The case of a 5-year-old black girl in Florida comes to mind, who in 2005 was handcuffed and arrested by three police officers after throwing a tantrum in class. The public response to the shocking tape of her arrest ranged from blame directed toward the police and the school principal—to blame directed at the child and her family. Many comments below the You-Tube video of her arrest featured racist attacks. But other than legal action pursued by her family, public outcry was tempered.

When another little black girl, 6-year-old Desre'e Watson was arrested in her kindergarten class in Florida two years later for a similar classroom tantrum, she was booked in the Highland County jail and charged with a felony and two misdemeanors. On the other hand, when Zachary Christie, a white 6-year-old, was suspended from first grade and faced 45 days in an alternative school for troublemakers for taking a combination knife/fork/spoon to school, the widespread public outrage that followed led the school board to change the penalty for all young students to a three to five day suspension.

Zachary's punishment called into question harsh school "zero-tolerance" policies, and led to a change of policy in the local system. The cases of the two little black girls who became involved in the criminal justice system for throwing tantrums in kindergarten did not impact policy or practice.

In order to deconstruct who is detained and why in a local juvenile justice system, those who make such decisions—including schools, the police, juvenile court judges, and prosecutors—must have the courage to examine how their juvenile justice apparatus operates, and what impacts their decisions. Are their reactions to youth of color driven by fear, politics, anecdote and beliefs—or by data and informed analysis? We have found in our work that examining how decision-making points impact youth of color is an unnatural task for a local juvenile justice system to undertake. It is a shock to the institution. For that reason, there is an overall lack of accountability.

> *On any given day, more than 90,000 youth are in custody of the juvenile justice system. A majority of them are youth of color who are held for nonviolent offenses.*

Society Suffers as a Whole

On any given day, more than 90,000 youth are in custody of the juvenile justice system. A majority of them are youth of color who are held for nonviolent offenses. For this, our society pays a high moral and financial price. A recently issued Justice Policy Institute report found that states spend approximately $5.7 billion each year imprisoning youth, although it has been shown that nonviolent youth can be supervised safely in the community with alternatives that cost substantially less than incarceration and that could lower recidivism by up to 22 percent. Studies show that incarcerated youth are less likely than those in alternative programs to graduate from high school, are more likely to be unemployed as adults, and are more likely to be arrested and imprisoned as adults.

Tragic cases that receive widespread attention, such as the beating death of 16-year-old Derrion Albert in Chicago, are horrific, but also rare. While some youth involved in serious or violent crime should be detained for public safety, the more than two-thirds of detained youth are charged with property offenses, public order offenses, or status offenses (i.e. running away or breaking curfew). Why is this so? Simply put, as a society we do not demand nor expect excellence, fairness, rationality or accountability from our child-serving justice systems. This should no longer be acceptable. There is too much at stake for our democratic principles and our ability to compete in a global knowledge-based world.

I am no economist or futurist, but I know that as a country we are not well-served when we have so many uneducated youth of color lost in a juvenile justice apparatus that dictates when they should eat, shower and exercise—then released to the world without much hope for turning their lives around through higher education or work. We can do better. But in order to do so we must demand accountability from juvenile justice systems early and often.

Today, let us begin by eliminating life in prison without the possibility of parole for children who have not taken a life.

12

California Is Unjust in Sentencing Juveniles

Human Rights Watch

Human Rights Watch is an organization focused on protecting the rights of people around the world.

Among the statistics found in a 2008 study completed by Human Rights Watch is that while there are approximately 2,380 people in the United States currently serving life without parole for crimes committed when they were minors, there are only 7 throughout the rest of the world. In California alone, more than half of the youth sentenced are first time offenders with no previous criminal record. The Human Rights Watch survey of these inmates also found that many had not actually committed the murder and that their adult codefendants actually received a lesser sentence. While other states are taking steps to eliminate this harsh sentence, California has made no attempt at reform.

Approximately 227 youth have been sentenced to die in California's prisons. They have not been sentenced to death: the death penalty was found unconstitutional for juveniles by the United States Supreme Court in 2005. Instead, these young people have been sentenced to prison for the rest of their lives, with no opportunity for parole and no chance for release. Their crimes were committed when they were teenagers, yet they will die in prison. Remarkably, many of the adults who were codefendants and took part in their crimes received lower sentences and will one day be released from prison.

Those who cannot buy cigarettes or alcohol, sign a rental agreement, or vote are nevertheless considered culpable to the same degree as an adult when they commit certain crimes and face adult penalties. Many feel life without parole is the equivalent of a death sentence. "They said a kid can't get the death penalty, but life without, it's the same thing. I'm condemned ... I don't understand the difference," said Robert D., now 32 years of age, serving a life without parole sentence for a crime he committed in high school. He participated in a robbery in which his codefendant unexpectedly shot the victim.

[Juvenile] life without parole allows no chance for a young person to change and to prove that change has occurred.

The California law permitting juveniles to be sentenced to life without parole for murder was enacted in 1990. Since that time, advances in neuroscience have found that adolescents and young adults continue to develop in ways particularly relevant to assessing criminal behavior and an individual's ability to be rehabilitated. Much of the focus on this relatively new discovery has been on teenagers' limited comprehension of risk and consequences, and the inability to act with adult-like volition. Just as important, however, is the conclusion that teens are still developing. These findings show that young offenders are particularly amenable to change and rehabilitation. For most teens, risk-taking and criminal behavior is fleeting; they cease with maturity. California's sentencing of youth to life without parole allows no chance for a young person to change and to prove that change has occurred.

Prejudice Against Offenders of Color

In California, it is not just the law itself that is out of step with international norms and scientific knowledge. The state's application of the law is also unjust. Eighty-five percent of youth sentenced to life without parole are people of color, with 75 percent of all cases in California being African American or Hispanic youth. African American youth are sentenced to life without parole at a rate that is 18.3 times the rate for whites. Hispanic youth in California are sentenced to life without parole at a rate that is five times the rate of white youth in the state.

California has the worst record in the country for racially disproportionate sentencing. In California, African American youth are sentenced to life without parole at rates that suggest unequal treatment before sentencing courts. This unequal treatment by sentencing courts cannot be explained only by white and African American youths' differential involvement in crime.

Adult Influences Not Punished as Harshly

Significantly, many of these crimes are committed by youth under an adult's influence. Based on survey responses and other case information, we estimate that in nearly 70 percent of California cases, when juveniles committed their crime with codefendants, at least one of these codefendants was an adult. Acting under the influence and, in some cases, the direction of an adult, however, cannot be considered a mitigating factor by the sentencing judge in California. In fact, the opposite appears to be true. Juveniles with an adult codefendant are typically more harshly treated than the adult. In over half of the cases in which there was an adult codefendant, the adult received a lower sentence than the juvenile.

Poor Legal Representation

Poor legal representation often compromises a just outcome in juvenile life without parole cases. Many interviewees told us that they participated in their legal proceedings with little understanding of what was happening. "I didn't even know I got [life without parole] until I talked to my lawyer after the hear-

ing," one young man said. Furthermore, in nearly half th
California cases surveyed, respondents to Human Rights Watch
reported that their own attorney did not ask the court for a
lower sentence. In addition, attorneys failed to prepare youth
for sentencing and did not tell them that a family member or
other person could speak on their behalf at the sentencing
hearing. In 68 percent of cases, the sentencing hearings pro-
ceeded with no witness speaking for the youth.

While some family members of victims support the sentence of life without parole for juveniles, the perspective of
victims is not monolithic. Interviews with the families of victims who were murdered by teens show the complex and
multi-faceted beliefs of those most deeply affected. Some families of victims believe that sentencing a young person to a
sentence of life without parole is immoral.

Public awareness about this issue has increased.

California Needs to Reform Its Policy

California's policy to lock up youth offenders for the rest of
their lives comes with a significant financial cost: the current
juvenile life without parole population will cost the state approximately half a billion dollars by the end of their lives.
This population and the resulting costs will only grow as
more youth are sentenced to spend the rest of their lives in
prison.

California is not the only state that sentences youth to life
without parole. Thirty-eight others apply the sentence as well.
However, movement to change these laws is occurring across
the country. Legislative efforts are pending in Florida, Illinois,
and Michigan and there are grassroots movements in Iowa,
Louisiana, Massachusetts, Nebraska, and Washington. Most recently, Colorado outlawed life without parole for children in
2006.

If life without parole for youth under age 18 were eliminated in California, other existing state law provides ample protection for public safety. California's next harshest penalty for murder secures a minimum of 25 years in prison. There are no reductions in the minimum time served for a murder conviction. Even then, parole is merely an option and won only through the prisoner's demonstrating rehabilitation. If they do earn release after 25 years or more, they are statistically unlikely to commit a new crime of any type. Prisoners released after serving a sentence for a murder have the lowest recidivism rate of all prisoners.

Public awareness about this issue has increased recently through newspaper and magazine articles and television coverage. With a significant number of the country's juvenile life without parole cases in its prisons, California has the opportunity to help lead the nation by taking immediate steps to change this unnecessarily harsh sentencing law.

13

Massachusetts Is Too Harsh in Sentencing Juveniles

Jonathan Saltzman

Jonathan Saltzman has been the legal affairs reporter for the Boston Globe *since 2003.*

Studies performed by the Children's Law Center of Massachusetts has shown that Massachusetts is among the states with the toughest juvenile laws. Most of the people sentenced to life without parole in the state were first-time offenders. The current law in Massachusetts treats children as young as fourteen as adults, sentencing them to life with no chance of parole. This is attributed by some to the overreaction of some policy makers to rare, horrific crimes committed by a few juveniles. There is also a possible racial disparity in the Massachusetts justice system, with 47 percent of juveniles sentenced to life without parole being black. Despite these statistics and the gradual decline in juvenile crime, the state is still slow to review its policy.

Despite its liberal reputation, Massachusetts has one of the harshest laws in the country for sentencing murderers as young as 14 to life in prison without parole, and many of the 57 people serving such mandatory sentences are first-time offenders, according to an advocacy group that wants them to become eligible for parole.

The Children's Law Center of Massachusetts, in what it said was the first comprehensive study of the 1996 law that re-

Jonathan Saltzman, "Juvenile Life-Without-Parole Sentence Too Harsh, Reports Says," *The Boston Globe*, September 30, 2009. Reproduced by permission.

sulted in such sentences for first-degree murder, found that a disproportionate percentage of the children locked up for the rest of their lives are black. Many of the offenders were convicted with adult codefendants, some of whom got milder sentences and have been freed.

Treating Children Like Adults Is Wrong

The report . . . followed a two-year review of most of the cases in which children ages 14, 15, and 16 were tried in adult court and sentenced to life. The study says that penalties for juvenile murderers were inadequate in the 1980s but that the Legislature went too far when it passed the current law in response to what the center describes as overblown fears of young super predators.

The group wants Governor Deval Patrick and the Legislature to change the law to at least make juveniles convicted of first-degree murder eligible for parole after 15 years, as is true for people convicted of second-degree murder.

"Life-without-parole sentences may be an appropriate response to some adult crimes, especially in a state like Massachusetts that does not impose the death penalty," the 33-page report said. "But the current law treats youths as young as 14 exactly like adults, regardless of their age, past conduct, level of participation in the crime, personal background, and potential for rehabilitation."

Geline W. Williams, executive director of the Massachusetts District Attorneys Association, said she could not comment on the report until she reads it. But, "there's no question that there are some juveniles who commit absolutely horrific crimes and have absolutely horrific records before they commit the ultimate crime of murder," she said.

The two state lawmakers who chair the joint Committee on the Judiciary, Representative Eugene L. O'Flaherty and Senator Cynthia Stone Creem, said they were willing to reexamine the 1996 law.

O'Flaherty said a few notorious crimes can often result in "legislative overreaction, and usually it takes a few years to see the unforeseen consequences of getting too tough, too quickly, and not being smart about getting tough."

Forty percent of the offenders had been convicted along with adult defendants, but many of the adults got lighter sentences.

Other States Are Considering Reform

Massachusetts is one of at least 39 states with youths serving sentences of life without parole; about 2,500 inmates around the country serve such sentences. But only Massachusetts and Connecticut give adult courts exclusive jurisdiction over murder cases against children as young as 14 and then impose a mandatory life-without-parole sentence for all first-degree murder convictions, regardless of the circumstances, the report said.

Several states are considering changing their laws to give youth offenders an opportunity to earn parole, in part because scientific research into the difference between the adolescent and adult brain shows that teenagers often cannot appreciate the consequences of their actions.

Last year [2008], after citing similar neuroscientific evidence, Human Rights Watch called sentences of life without parole for juveniles "cruel, unfair, and unnecessary."

Massachusetts enacted the current law, partly in response to insufficient juvenile court sentences in the 1980s, when the harshest punishment for a juvenile who was not transferred to an adult court—even for murder—was incarceration until 21.

In the 1990s, a number of widely publicized juvenile murder cases prompted the Legislature to mandate that all juveniles charged with first- or second-degree murder be tried in adult court and that conviction for first-degree murder result in an automatic sentence of life without parole.

81

One of those cases involved Edward S. O'Brien, the 15-year-old who stabbed his best friend's mother 98 times across the street from his Somerville home in 1995. After two years of hearings and intervention by the state's highest court, O'Brien was tried as an adult and sentenced to life without parole.

The Children's Law Center contends that crime rates do not justify such harsh sentences. Homicide rates for Massachusetts youth under 18 peaked in 1992.

Since 1998, the homicide rate among adolescents has been lower than it was 30 years ago.

Adults Get Off Easier

The center, which reviewed in detail 46 of the 57 juvenile murderers serving life sentences without parole, said 41 percent had no prior record. Forty percent of the offenders had been convicted along with adult defendants, but many of the adults got lighter sentences.

"Frequently, the adults who are actually the primary actors [in the murders] and are in possession of the knowledge that matters are in a better position to offer information in exchange for better treatment from prosecutors," said Lia Monahon, the lawyer for the center who wrote the report.

Blacks make up 47 percent of the juveniles sentenced to life without parole but account for less than 7 percent of children under 18 in Massachusetts, said the report. Monahon said the disparity could reflect bias in the criminal justice system.

14

Juvenile LWOP Wastes Taxpayer Money

Eartha Jane Melzer

Eartha Jane Melzer covers environmental and social issues in the state of Michigan for the Michigan Messenger, *an independent newsmagazine.*

Not only is sentencing youth to life without parole (LWOP) unethical, but it also has a negative impact on taxpayers. With most of these prisoners still in their youth, it is estimated that these sentences could cost taxpayers millions over the next several decades. This money could be better spent on preventive programs earlier in life before these young people actually have the chance to turn to a life of crime.

Michigan's prison system holds 346 inmates who are serving life without parole for crimes they committed as children. As the state struggles with a $1.5 billion deficit and a prison system that eats up 20 percent of the budget, a bill to end the controversial practice of sending minors to prison for life may gain momentum in the state Legislature.

The United States is the only nation that allows life without parole for juvenile offenders and, according to a report by Human Rights Watch, Michigan ranks third among states for number of people serving such sentences.

Old Legislation Needs to Be Updated

Shelli Weisberg, legislative director for the American Civil Liberties Union of Michigan, an advocate for banning mandatory

Eartha Jane Melzer, "Juveniles Sentenced to Life Without Parole Cost the State Millions," *The Michigan Messenger*, February 24, 2009. Reproduced by permission.

life sentences for children, explained that Michigan's large number of juvenile lifers is a result of legislation enacted in the 1980s during a period of fear about a wave of juvenile crime.

"People were worried about 'super predators,'" she said. "States around the country started really cracking down, with laws that were intended to get the worst of the worst—kids so far gone that there is nothing that can help them."

But the fear was a scare tactic, Weisberg said. "In fact the juvenile crime wave was temporary and has gone down."

In a third of the cases in which Michigan juveniles are sentenced to life without parole, she said, the crime is their first offense.

But tough-on-crime laws beginning in 1988 mandated life without parole sentences for certain crimes, and allowed children as young as 14 to be tried as an adult without a special hearing.

The current law that prohibits rehabilitation and release will cost the state hundreds of millions of dollars over the next several decades.

New Ideas Are Being Considered

Legislation introduced this month [February 2009] by state Sen. Liz Brater (D-Ann Arbor), which has been referred to the Senate Judiciary Committee, would ban life without parole for juveniles. It would also allow those already serving mandatory life sentences for crimes committed as juveniles to apply for parole after a portion of their sentence is served.

"It is inhumane and it is inappropriate to take children before their brains are fully developed and subject them to the same sentence that adults would get," Brater said. "Many of them were sentenced along with an adult defender who got a lesser sentence and many of these youth were victims of abuse or neglect in their homes or are people with mental illness or disability."

The Cost to the Taxpayers

In addition to the ethical problems, she said, incarcerating young people for their full lives represents a significant expenditure for taxpayers and this money could probably do more to prevent crime if spent earlier in life on services like preschool.

It costs at least $30,000 per year to keep an inmate in the state prison system, according to the Department of Corrections. With 346 mostly still-young lifers serving time for juvenile crime, the current law that prohibits rehabilitation and release will cost the state hundreds of millions of dollars over the next several decades.

Brater, who has introduced this same legislation in the last two legislative sessions, said that she feels it has developed some momentum. Last year [in 2008] the House held a hearing on the legislation and then passed it with strong bipartisan support.

Gary Walker is president of the Michigan Prosecutors Association, a group that has historically opposed bills to end mandatory life sentences for juveniles.

Determining an Appropriate Age

The legislation proposed by Brater could represent a "monumental change in terms" for the Michigan criminal justice system, Walker said, because the general age of criminal responsibility is 17 in Michigan and a large number of criminal offenses are committed by people between 17 and 18 years old.

In Michigan, as in 13 other states, people who are 17 years old are considered adults by the criminal justice system, Walker said. Prosecutors have the option of charging younger offenders as juveniles, Walker said, and generally charge them as adults only in cases involving "horrific" crimes.

The legislation to end juvenile life without parole would in effect change the age of criminal responsibility to 18, Walker said.

"There is no real magic to the age of responsibility," he said. Some people as young as 16 are fully aware of the meaning of their actions and decades ago the age of majority was 21.

"If we were to be starting out now, 18 may well be an appropriate choice."

Walker said that Michigan prosecutors are open to working with the legislation's supporters.

"We are always willing to discuss legislation and we try to shape it in a way that is appropriate to Michigan citizens," he said. "I want to see the kids in caps and gowns, not in jump suits."

Organizations to Contact

The editors have compiled the following list of organizations concerned with the issues debated in this book. The descriptions are derived from materials provided by the organizations. All have publications or information available for interested readers. The list was compiled on the date of publication of the present volume: information provided here may change. Be aware that many organizations take several weeks or longer to respond to inquiries, so allow as much time as possible for the receipt of requested materials.

American Civil Liberties Union
125 Broad St., 18th Floor, New York, NY   10004
(212) 549-2500
website: www.aclu.org

Founded in 1920, the American Civil Liberties Union fights to defend and protect the rights of all Americans in the courts, legislatures, and communities. Its mission is to ensure that everyone is given equal rights, as the Constitution states, and to expand this guarantee to the minority issues that have been excluded in the past.

Center for Children's Law and Policy
1701 K St. NW, Suite 1100, Washington, DC   20006
(202) 637-0377 • fax: (202) 379-1600
e-mail: info@cclp.org
website: www.cclp.org

The Center for Children's Law and Policy focuses on the reform of juvenile justice and other systems involving at-risk children and protecting the rights of the children in these systems. It plays a major role in foundation-funded juvenile justice initiatives, supporting reform work in more than twenty jurisdictions across the United States.

Center on Juvenile and Criminal Justice
440 Ninth St., San Francisco, CA   94103
(415) 621-5661 • fax: (415) 621-5466
website: www.cjcj.org

The Center on Juvenile and Criminal Justice was established in 1985 as a nonprofit nonpartisan organization fighting for a fair and humane criminal justice system. It provides direct services, such as support and reentry programs for parolees; technical assistance, such as state-to-state case management; and policy analysis. Its senior staff members possess more than thirty years of experience in the criminal justice field, and the organization is among the leading criminal justice agencies nationwide.

Child Rights Information Network
East Studio, 2, Pontypool Place, London, SE1 8QF
   United Kingdom
+44 20 7401 2257
e-mail: info@crin.org
website: www.crin.org

Child Rights Information Network has a vision of a world where all children have access to equal human rights. Its goal is to build a global network for children's rights by advocating for a change in how governments and societies view children. It also leads advocacy campaigns, international children's rights coalitions, and efforts to make human rights enforcement tools available to everyone. Several of its resources are available for download directly from the website.

Coalition for Juvenile Justice
1710 Rhode Island Ave. NW, 10th Floor
Washington, DC   20036
(202) 467-0864 • fax: (202) 887-0738
e-mail: info@juvjustice.org
website: www.juvjustice.org

Founded in 2005, the Coalition for Juvenile Justice is a national nonprofit organization that represents governor-appointed advisory groups on juvenile justice in the United

States and the District of Columbia. Its goals are to ensure the fair treatment of children and families and to ensure juvenile offenders are provided the resources to become productive members of their communities. It promotes policies to reduce and prevent delinquency, educates the public on urgent matters regarding juvenile justice, and brings together national, state, and local advocates and organizations.

Crime Victims Action Alliance
1809 S St., #101316, Sacramento, CA   95811
(916) 273-3603 • toll-free fax: (888) 235-7067
e-mail: information@cvactionalliance.org
website: www.cvactionalliance.org

The Crime Victims Action Alliance is a nonprofit organization working to promote victims' rights and public safety. It advocates for the improvement of laws, regulations, and policies, and its vision is of a justice system that is centered on the victim and their families. Since its inception in 1992, it has played an important role in the passage of bills and initiatives that improve the lives of victims and their families. Its website offers the most up-to-date news on ever-changing laws and policies, as well as a list of publications that offer more information.

Equal Justice Initiative
122 Commerce St., Montgomery, AL   36104
(334) 269-1803 • fax: (334) 269-1806
e-mail: contact_us@eji.org
website: www.eji.org

The Equal Justice Initiative is a private nonprofit organization that represents a variety of individuals that have been treated unjustly by the legal system. It also works with communities most affected by poverty and unequal treatment. In its effort to reform the criminal justice system, it prepares reports, newsletters, and manuals to aid advocates and policy makers in their decisions regarding the laws. The website provides current news information as well as an abundance of resources.

Juvenile Justice Initiative
518 Davis St., Suite 211, Evanston, IL   60201
(847) 864-1567
e-mail: bcjuv@aol.com
website: www.jjustice.org

The Juvenile Justice Initiative was founded in 2000 upon its receiving funding from the John D. and Catherine T. Mac-Arthur Foundation and the Woods Fund of Chicago. It is a nonprofit, nonpartisan statewide coalition that includes state and local organizations, legal educators, and child advocates as well as many others. Its mission is the transformation of the juvenile justice system into a more fair and equal system and to reduce the reliance on the detention of youths.

Juvenile Law Center
1315 Walnut St., 4th Floor, Philadelphia, PA   19107
(215) 625-0551 • fax: (215) 625-2808
website: www.jlc.org

The Juvenile Law Center was founded in 1975 as a nonprofit legal service for children and is one of the oldest multi-issue public-interest law firms in the United States. Its mission is to protect and promote juveniles' rights in the justice and child welfare systems. Some of the actions it takes to achieve its goals are training judges, lawyers, and other professionals; educating the public on key issues; and advocating for juvenile justice and child welfare reform. An outline of its plans for 2009–2011 is available on its website.

National Center for Juvenile Justice (NCJJ)
3700 S. Water St., Suite 200, Pittsburgh, PA   15203
(412) 227-6950 • fax: (412) 227-6955
e-mail: ncjj@ncjj.org
website: www.ncjj.org

The National Center for Juvenile Justice was established in 1973 as a research organization that conducts research on crime and delinquency on a national and subnational level.

Since its formation, it has developed resources rendering it a valuable resource in the field of juvenile justice. Its mission is to provide effective justice for children and families through its research and assistance.

National Center for Youth Law

405 Fourteenth St., 15th Floor, Oakland, CA 94612
(510) 835-8098 • fax: (510) 835-8099
e-mail: info@youthlaw.org
website: www.youthlaw.org

The National Center for Youth Law's mission is to ensure that low-income children are provided the same access to legal counsel and services as those with higher incomes. It works to promote programs, laws, and policies that encourage a better future for these juveniles. It achieves its goals by providing training to foster parents, attorneys, and others; assisting legal advocates who represent poor children; and by publishing articles, books, and the quarterly journal *Youth Law News*.

National Council of Juvenile and Family Court Judges

PO Box 8970, Reno, NV 89507
(775) 784-6012 • fax: (775) 784-6628
e-mail: staff@ncjfcj.org
website: www.ncjfcj.org

Founded in 1937, the National Council of Juvenile and Family Court Judges strives to provide judges, courts, and other agencies involved in juvenile and family law the information needed to ensure fair and effective justice for children and families. Its mission is to improve the courts and legal systems and raise awareness of the major issues affecting children and families today, such as domestic violence and child abuse. It achieves this goal by providing training to more than thirty thousand judges, court administrators, and social and mental health professionals as well as and many others involved in this field.

National Organization of Victims of Juvenile Lifers

PO Box 498, Davisburg, MI   48350
(847) 446-7073
e-mail: novjl@aol.com
website: www.jlwopvictims.org

The National Organization of Victims of Juvenile Lifers is dedicated to ensuring that victims and their families' voices are heard in the debate on whether or not to abolish juvenile life without parole sentences. Along with advocating for the victims, it offers a wealth of information on its website, such as victims' stories, up-to-date news, and documents that provide additional information.

Office of Juvenile Justice and Delinquency Prevention (OJJDP)

810 Seventh St. NW, Washington, DC   20531
(202) 307-5911
website: www.ojjdp.gov

The Office of Juvenile Justice and Delinquency Prevention, a component of the US Department of Justice, is a national program working to prevent juvenile delinquency and victimization. It provides communities nationwide with the resources to develop and implement prevention and intervention programs, as well as to improve the juvenile justice system. Its goal is to develop solutions and programs suited to the needs of juveniles and their families while holding the offender responsible for his actions and keeping public safety a priority.

Sentencing Project

1705 DeSales St. NW, 8th Floor, Washington, DC   20036
(202) 628-0871 • fax: (202) 628-1091
e-mail: staff@sentencingproject.org
website: www.sentencingproject.org

The Sentencing Project is a national organization founded in 1986 with the goal of reducing the dependence on incarceration as criminal punishment. Since then it has expanded its mission to champion reforms in sentencing laws and practice, as well as to promoting alternatives to incarceration. It achieves its goal through making its research available to the public and by educating people on the issues that need to change within the justice system.

Bibliography

Books

John Aarons, Lisa Smith, and Linda Wagner	*Dispatches from Juvenile Hall: Fixing a Failing System.* New York: Penguin, 2009.
Clemens F. Bartollas and Stuart J. Miller	*Voices in the Juvenile Justice System for Juvenile Justice in America.* Upper Saddle River, NJ: Prentice-Hall, 2007.
David Chura	*I Don't Wish Nobody to Have a Life Like Mine: Tales of Kids in Adult Lock Up.* Boston: Beacon, 2010.
Michael A. Corriero	*Judging Children as Children: A Proposal for a Juvenile Justice System.* Philadelphia: Temple University Press, 2007.
Anne-Marie Cusac	*Cruel and Unusual: The Culture of Punishment in America.* New Haven, CT: Yale University Press, 2009.
Debbie J. Goodman and Ron Grimming	*Juvenile Justice: A Collection of True-Crime Cases.* Upper Saddle River, NJ: Prentice-Hall, 2007.
Clayton A. Hartjen	*Youth, Crime, and Justice: A Global Inquiry.* Piscataway, NJ: Rutgers University Press, 2008.
John Hubner	*Last Chance in Texas: The Redemption of Criminal Youth.* New York: Random House Trade Paperbacks, 2008.

Richard Lawrence   *School Crime and Juvenile Justice.* New York: Oxford University Press, 2007.

Anne M. Nurse   *Locked Up, Locked Out: Young Men in the Juvenile Justice System.* Nashville: Vanderbilt University Press, 2010.

Rick Ruddell and Matthew O. Thomas   *Juvenile Corrections.* Richmond, KY: Newgate, 2009.

Laurie Schaffner   *Girls in Trouble with the Law.* Piscataway, NJ: Rutgers University Press, 2006.

Elizabeth S. Scott and Laurence Steinburg   *Rethinking Juvenile Justice.* Cambridge, MA: Harvard University Press, 2008.

Periodicals and Internet Sources

Robert Barnes   "Supreme Court Restricts Life Without Parole for Juveniles," *Washington Post,* May 18, 2010.

Emily Bazelon   "They're Just Kids," *Slate,* May 17, 2010.

Lewis Beale   "Should Minors Ever Face Life Without Parole?" *Miller-McCune,* July 7, 2009.

Jean Casella and James Ridgeway   "Supreme Court Decision Limits Juvenile Life Without Parole (Within Limits)," *Solitary Watch,* May 17, 2010.

David Chura   "Cruel and Unusual
                         Punishment—Minors Locked Up for
                         Life Without Parole," *Red Room*,
                         November 27, 2009.

Ben Conery   "Justices Weigh Juveniles' Life
                         Without Parole," *Washington Times*,
                         November 10, 2009.

Lloyd   "Florida Justice: Tough on Youths,"
Dunkelberger   *Sarasota (FL) Herald-Tribune*, August
                         9, 2009.

Jeffrey Fagan   "Myths of Get-Tough Law," *St.
                         Petersburg (FL) Times*, November 2,
                         2009.

Earl Ofari   "Life Without Parole for Teens Is
Hutchinson   Uncivilized," *New America Media*,
                         November 27, 2009.

Adam Liptak   "Weighing Life in Prison for Youths
                         Who Didn't Kill," *New York Times*,
                         November 7, 2009.

Trey Lyon   "Do Teenage Criminals Deserve Life
                         Without Parole?" EthicsDaily.com,
                         November 18, 2009.

Eartha Jane   "As Bill to Ban Life Imprisonment
Melzer   for Children Languishes, Inequities of
                         Defense Persist," *Michigan Messenger*,
                         April 13, 2009.

Tolu Olorunda   "Sarah Kruzan: 16-Year-Old
                         Sentenced to Life for Killing Pimp,"
                         Daily Voice, October 26, 2009.

Ed Pilkington   "Life Without Hope," *Guardian* (Manchester, UK), August 4, 2007.

Claudia Rowe   "A Look at Why State Teens Can Get Life Without Parole," *Seattle Post-Intelligencer,,* February 5, 2009.

Debra Saunders   "Keep Life Without Parole, Life After Death," *Real Clear Politics*, August 2, 2009.

Elizabeth S. Scott and Laurence Steinburg   "The Young and the Restless," *New York Times*, November 13, 2009.

Liliana Segura   "Major Supreme Court Ruling: Kids Who Didn't Kill Anyone Should Not Have to Die in Prison," *AlterNet*, May 18, 2010.

Ken Stier   "Getting the Juvenile-Justice System to Grow Up," *Time*, March 24, 2009.

Charles D. Stimson   "Adult Time for Adult Crime: Manufacturing Statistics for 19-year-old 'Juveniles,'" *Foundry*, October 22, 2009.

Cal Thomas   "Life for Children," *Washington Times*, November 26, 2009.

Index